Dedication

This book is dedicated to our beautiful planet Mother Earth; and all who dwell upon her.

The Way Forward 2

Reviews

"Dear Lindsay, thank you so much for your interpretation of the changing energies of Mother Earth and our transition into the New Golden Age.

Your second book "*The Way Forward 2*" is written in line with these changing energies, and through The Crystal Team you have been able to communicate how the world around us, and nature itself, is complementing and supporting us as we all move into the New Golden Age, returning to the qualities of living within the Atlantean frequencies.

I believe this book is written in a way that we can all understand as it shares with us knowledge that is crucial to opening our awareness of the changing world around and within us.

Using our crystals during the coming years will help us to evolve with ease and grace as we allow them to support us, and share their abundant knowledge about living life in the new evolving World".

Katy Gostick: Mission for Peace, Spiritual Facilitator, Healer

"*The Way Forward - Understanding the World around You*" is an exciting new book that will lift the reader's energy vibrations so making them aware of a higher way of being and living. Lindsay is wholeheartedly dedicated to helping others through her work which is manifested in this great thought-provoking book.

Margaret Merrison: The Unicorn Centre for Spiritual Learning, Author

Contents

Introduction from The Crystal Team

PART I

Magnificent Energies Granted	5
Coming Home	8
The Significance of 12-12-12	11
Celebrating 12-12-12	13
Unification of Energies	14
The Significance of 21-12-12	16
Celebrating 21-12-12	19
Celebrations around the World on 21-12-12	20
2013 – The Dawn of a New Era	23
Acting with Integrity	24
The Crystal World	28
Spreading the Light and Love	31
144 Crystalline Grid	35
Living in Joy and Harmony	37
Laughter – A Priceless Gift	39
Peace on Earth	41
A Beautiful Meditation for Peace on Earth	42
Prayer for Peace	43
Spirits of Pure Love	44
Life in Other Dimensions	46
Clearing Your Energetic Imbalances	48
The Energy of Your Name	50
A Gift from God Indeed	53
Bringing in the Feminine Energies	54
Messengers from the Angelic Realms	55
The Tree Kingdom	60
Music	61
Trees – the Lungs of the Planet	62

Insights on Communication	65
Insights on Crop Circles	70
Colours of Light	71
Experiencing Heaven on Earth	74
Insights from the Sea-World	76
The Beauty of Life	78
This Thing Called Love	80
The Light of God	83
Crystals Hold the Secrets of all Life	85
Simple Prayers	87
Connecting to the Energies of Love (meditation)	88
The Grace of God	91
The Body's Ability to Heal Itself through Self-Communication	93
The Way Forward to Peace on Earth is Now Set	97
A Few More Words on Love	99
Insights on Animal Communication (Dogs)	102
Pyramids – a Link between Heaven and Earth	109
A Message of Joy	113
A State of Grace	115
Connecting to the Christ Consciousness	119
Opening Your Heart Centre (meditation)	120
Insights on Colours of Lights	121
The Pink and Silver Flame	125
Maintaining Soul Connection	127
Insights on the Animal Kingdom (Cats)	129
Time for Reflection for the New Year Ahead	133
See Love in all Things	136
Your Right of Passage	137
Intention and Purpose	139
Creative Solutions	142
Insights on the Animal Kingdom (Butterflies)	146
A Meditation to align you with the Love and Heart Energies of God	149

PART II

Circle of Love	152
Trinity Healing & Prayer Circle	153
Crystal Skull World Day	155
Centre for Peaceful Restoration, Recovery and Recuperation	157
About Lindsay	159
Contact Lindsay	160
Acknowledgements	161
Index	165

The Way Forward 2 - Foreword

Words of love, guidance, support and encouragement are offered, to demonstrate the unfolding of the Divine Plan, laid down for you all eons of time ago.

Insights reveal the multitude of signs and assistance available to us, to understand all that is being made available to us, and to help us move closer to the light and love of God.

This love that withstands all, that understands all, and shines brightly for you all to come home to at the end of this physical existence you have chosen at this time.

Through understanding the world around you, we gain insights into living in harmony with All That Is, with each other, with Mother Earth, with all living beings, and this is an important part of our learning and discovery at this time.

Information on crystals, demonstrates the magnificence of these powerful beings, and the role they have the potential to play in the future of all humanity, and linking to these amazing energies will increase the understanding and awareness of all souls at this time, helping them to make a stronger connection to Source, and understand their own true path and purpose in this existence.

The energies of love, compassion, understanding, acceptance and goodwill, come through these words and insights in the most beautiful way, to help move us into the new energies, the new dimension of the future, the new Golden Age on Earth.

Introduction from The Crystal Team

"It is our great delight and joy to offer words of introduction to this powerful and inspiring collection of insights and information.

Our purpose in offering these words and energies is to enable you to understand the world around you, to understand that we are all part of one whole unit; we are all part of the same, although individual in our own unique way.

Working as a whole, understanding the principle of oneness, will help you to see that each action has a resulting action, and that positive thoughts, actions, deeds and intentions will result in positive outcomes for all humanity, all living beings, Mother Earth and out into the universe and beyond. And understanding this, words are offered to explain how all aspects of life seen and unseen, understood and not understood, are a vital part in all of this bigger picture, and so communications and energies from all aspects of life on this planet and beyond are an integral part of the whole; so information on communications from other life forms beyond your planet, on crop circles, communications from birds, dolphins and other animals are included along with aspects of other living beings in nature such as trees and flowers.

For all these aspects, dear ones are part of the energy system, part of the communication system, and part of the whole picture that makes up your world.

So in understanding how all parts fit together, are inter-related and inter-dependent, will demonstrate how all life forms and all aspects of your life must be treated and viewed as part of the whole, and negative intentions, deeds, thoughts and actions will result in negative outcomes throughout the whole of your earthly orbit and beyond into the realms of space.

We all have a responsibility, dear ones, to have an awareness and understanding of this bigger picture, for we all chose to experience life on this Earth; we all chose to experience life in a physical body at this exciting time on Earth. This time of great change and great potential, this time of moving forwards into the new time, the new dawn, the new Golden Age of love, peace, harmony, joy, and happiness.

In understanding all that God has made available to us, in understanding the depth and strength of the love of God, then you begin to understand all that is being made available to you. You understand all the help, assistance and love that is available to call on at all times to help you move into this new era of new times.

As each individual makes those choices that release all their past accumulated energies, that enables them to move into their own true path and purpose, to move further into the light and love of God, then they are playing their part in the unfolding of the Divine Plan, a Plan laid down for you all eons of time ago, a Plan laid down to assist at this special time on Earth, to move you, all living beings and Mother Earth forwards, into the new time of peace and harmony.

As each person moves forwards, so their energies inspire and ignite in others the remembrance of the ancient wisdom and knowledge that is held within all of us, within our cellular structure, our DNA and our crystalline grid.

As each action, thought, deed and intention demonstrates how beautifully life flows when you are in the energies of love and light, when you work with the flow of energies of peace and harmony, then you demonstrate the beauty of how life can be when all are open and aware of the gift of life, and this adventure that you are now part of.

As your light shines brighter, as your energies raise, then others will be drawn to you, to question, to be part of your energy emanations, and this will assist and encourage them to take those first steps to open and explore, to reunite with all that they inherently know and understand within each particle of their beingness.

And so as more people open, as their lights begin to shine, so the energies of Mother Earth lighten and clear and shine out brighter and clearer, and this helps her move forward in her journey too, for she is on her own adventure and will continue to move forward, and it will be easier for your humanity if they move forwards in alignment with her energies in peace and light and love.

And as Mother Earth is part of your solar system and this is part of the bigger picture of space, then so too her energies will shine brighter, and will be more harmonious with those of the outer reaches of space, and so all will be in alignment, and all will be peaceful and harmonious. For, dear ones remember that bigger picture that exists beyond your own orbit and that of Mother Earth, and all is part of one, and all is part of the same.

And so we leave you now to enjoy these words and energies. Read, absorb and integrate the energies, the love, the understanding and intentions of our words, dear ones, and this will help you in your understanding, in clearing your energies, and in moving forward in your own glorious adventure that you have chosen to experience at this special time in your history, and you will be fulfilling your part of the Plan laid down for you all, part of this glorious Plan for a wonderful existence that is being made available for you all, and remember dear ones, that you are truly and deeply loved at all times by the fount of all love, by the provider, Source, call it what you will, by the love of God who has made all this possible for you all.

With our greatest love, The Crystal Team."

PART I
Magnificent Energies Granted
6th and 7th October 2012

During 2012, the Divine Plan, laid down for us all eons of time ago, continued to unfold in all its glory. The Crystal Team joyously continue to communicate the love and assistance that is available to us all as part of the unfolding of this wonderful Plan, and their words of wisdom and inspiration assist us to move forward into the new era, the new Golden Age with joy and harmony, and empower us to become the true glorious beings that we truly are.

As part of the unfolding of this Divine Plan, information was offered indicating further significant events would take place during the weekend of 6th and 7th October 2012.

★★★★★★★★★★

"Our dear Earth friends, this weekend is indeed a very special event in this auspicious year of 2012 in your earthy timescale. The energies that are being sent down to this planet for the benefit of all living beings and Mother Earth are of the most brilliant, the most amazing light, bright, sparkly essence. These are being made available to you, as more and more of you are now awakening to your Atlantean and Lemurian energies, to that essence that is within you all and within your cellular structure and your DNA.

Celebrate the gift of these energies, breathe them in, allow them to integrate into your system, feel yourself lifted and raised up in these new glorious energies as part of the unfolding of the Divine Plan.

Relish this gift, dear ones, and feel the love and assistance that is available to you all, and know that all is well and all will be well, and we are here for you always to tune into as you progress on your journey through this Adventure called Life."

★★★★★★★★★★

Out walking on this special weekend along the beautiful South Devon coastline, I sensed the energies as clearer, cleaner, lighter and brighter. It was a perfect autumnal day, with warmth in the sunshine, the trees were just beginning to turn to a golden red and the clarity of the light was amazing. Within the brightness and lightness of the energies, there seemed more positivity, hope and joy. Other people also commented on the difference and sensed the beauty of the love and light being made available to us all.

I asked The Crystal Team for confirmation of the changing energies and they offered -

Confirmation from The Crystal Team

"The energies this weekend were indeed of the most beautiful and powerful that you can imagine, the brightness and lightness, the clarity and the very essence of light, love and joy became available to all those who choose to avail themselves.

Those of you on your journey to enlightenment, all light workers, peace workers, those who work with the energies of Mother Earth, those connected to the energies of the galaxies and constellations, all workers of love, light and peace, all those connecting to the Atlantean and Lemurian energies, all those who love and care for each other and all living beings and the planet, all those who want the best, the very best for all, those who seek the truth, the love of God, the light of God, and the bounty of all that is available to you all.

let go of all that holds you back

And so this beautiful, light and bright energy is not only wonderful to sense, feel and enjoy, it is being integrated into your cellular structure, your DNA, your very soul essence, your very core of love and joy, your connection to Source, your own truth and light, and as this energy is absorbed into your essence, it helps you to release those heavier energies that hold you back and prevent you from being the true glorious beings that you truly are; the heavier energies that keep you rooted in 3rd dimensional thinking, perception and actions and intentions.

You know you can feel the difference, dear ones, between when you feel light, bright, happy and joyful, optimistic, hopeful and energised compared to when you feel dense, heavy, down-hearted, worried, concerned, defeated and unhappy, and these are not energies that we wish you to feel, and so by releasing all those accumulated energies, you can let go of all that holds you back and prevents you from permanently being in a state of joy and happiness, at peace and in harmony with All That Is.

And this state, dear ones, is your natural state, like the Lemurians who were able to remain in a high frequency, remain in a state of love and joy, peace and harmony, as they avoided getting weighed down with the denser energies of life on Earth.

eternal soul growth

By remaining true to their purpose for experiencing life on Earth, by constantly reviewing and adjusting and accepting their boundaries, shall we say, of their remit for life on the earthly plane, then they remained in a state of lightness and brightness and joy. And so, dear ones, as those new energies are received and absorbed and integrated by each and every one of you, you can release all those past energies, thoughts, hurts, disappointments and other aspects that may keep or cause your energies to drop, to become heavier and denser, you can raise your energies to their true level of joy, lightness, happiness, brightness, peace and harmony, and live in this state of blissful energy.

For it is your choice, dear ones, this is why you have Free Will, this is why you came here to experience life on Earth, this is why you are here, dear ones, as another part of your eternal soul growth, to experience these energies and to make the choice to release these unwanted energies and to move forward in alignment with the changing energies of Mother Earth, for rest assured, she will move forward as part of her journey, and it will be much easier for her and your humanity if you move forward in alignment with these changing energies.

And so those powerful energies are offered to you now for you to blend, mix, integrate, absorb as part of your chosen path in this lifetime, for you to move forward in your true path and purpose in the unfolding of the magnificent Divine Plan laid down for you all by the loving God, the fount of all love, light, wisdom, knowledge and joy for you all.

We are pleased that many of you noticed an instant change in these energies and are able to enjoy the positivity and joy available to you; this will assist you all as the year moves forwards, this auspicious year of 2012, and so we watch with great joy, glee, happiness and excitement as all this unfolds in all its glory."

Coming Home

"We are always pleased to have the opportunity to work with you and offer information and energies that will be of great benefit to you all in this lifetime on the earthly plane.

As you approach the very special dates of 12-12-12, noticeable changes in the energy surrounding your earthly plane will be experienced and those who have been steadily adapting their energies to the new energies will move forwards more easily than those who have not yet fully accepted the opportunity to move forwards.

For all energies are changing on all levels, in all dimensions, because as you are aware we are all part of the same and are all part of one, so no one thing can change without a subsequent change in energies whether people have consciously chosen to change their energies or not. As your beautiful planet is part of the solar system, and that is part of the wider picture, then so too all consequent changes alter and adapt all energies around into the galaxies and constellations.

And, dear ones, this must happen in order for the implementation of the new era, the new Golden Age as part of the unfolding of the Divine Plan in all its glory.

light and love of unimaginable strength

And so, referring back to this special year and the two important dates in December, glorious changes will be occurring that have been laid down as part of the Plan – to enable the next parts of it to unfold for you all.

Aspects of this Plan are beyond your current understanding and comprehension so we will not confuse or complicate this for you at this time but as with the light flooding into the Earth Star Chakra after the brilliance of the Olympic and Paralympic Games*, so too light and love of unimaginable strength and power will be available to you all as this year unfolds.

It is a great time for celebrations, for gratitude and appreciation, for all that has been prepared for you all, and you are invited to welcome in these beautiful new energies which will help your life to flow more easily, more beautifully and more harmoniously. As more and more of you awaken to your Atlantean and Lemurian energies, as you reconnect to the glory of these Golden Ages, as you see how marvellous life can be when lived in joy and harmony, then this allows for more conscious awareness, more love, understanding, compassion and appreciation to enter your lives. As you raise your vibrations, in line with your true soul essence energy then life becomes joyful, easier, happier and more successful.

reconnecting to your role

By successful we do not wish to infer success measured by material gain or aggrandisement for this is harmful to yourself, to your soul energy, to Mother Earth and all living beings.

We do refer to success as 'coming home' as linking to those Atlantean and Lemurian energies, of reconnecting to your true path and purpose in this existence, of being at one with All That Is, of being and playing your role in the unfolding of this glorious Plan laid down for you all.

And as with Mother Earth agreeing to allow the growth of the crystals within her being for the benefit of the Atlantean technological growth and for them to be available for you all at this time, so too have you all agreed to play your part in the unfolding of the Divine Plan, so too have you all been aware on a soul level of what you came here to do, of what your purpose is in this glorious existence. And so as you reconnect to that energy, to that very purpose, you are reconnecting to your role, your agreement, your true path or reason for being here at this time, and how much more success can you wish to experience than that?

For many of you, the energies of this dimension are not easy to shed, as unlike the Lemurians who were able to remain in a very high frequency, many of you have become denser in your energy field and this will make it harder for you to lift your energies and reunite with your true path and purpose, but we encourage and invite you all, dear ones, to be prepared to move forward at this great shift in energies as we approach 21-12-12 for this will happen for certain and will be a lot easier for you if you are able to make that shift now.

We are here for you at all times, link into our powerful energies, ask for help to shift and move those stagnant energies so that you can benefit from and glory in the new light, bright, sparkly energies and feel your life flow more easily and joyfully.

we send our greatest love and encouragement."

* read more about this in the first in the series 'The Way Forward – Words of Wisdom, Inspiration, Information and Love' by Lindsay Ball.

The Significance of 12-12-12

As the exciting dates of 12-12-12 and 21-12-12 approached, I asked The Crystal Team for advice on the most appropriate place/s for me to visit on these special days. Their recommendation was for me to visit Avebury on 12-12-12 to link into the wonderful energies of the stone circle, and then to visit Glastonbury on 21-12-12 in order to consecrate those energies.

Preparing for my visit to Avebury, I asked for clarification on the potentialities of this special day, and for advice on how best to connect with the energies once at Avebury.

****

"This process taking its reality timeframe around the world, is of great significance to you all, and will create energies of light and love to lift all your energies towards those of the new dimension – the new era being made available to you all.

So we would welcome your energies in Avebury on 12-12-12; being in Avebury and walking around inviting the energies to open, to flow, to reconnect, to link and spread out in the most glorious way, forming those predetermined connections, forming those grids and securing in the light and the love, the appreciation, gratitude, honour and respect that has been waiting these moments in their history, to awaken now at this time in a joyful, harmonious symmetry of light and love.

the power of crystals

Link into the energies and be aware of the significance of the event and the energies being made available as part of the magnificent Divine Plan that has been laid down for you all. Be aware of the magnificence of the crystal energies, the power for good that they possess; how crystal power will be so significant in the future of your planet's progress and development.

Focus on the gift from God, the love and generosity of Mother Earth within this Plan, for it is all about co-operation and collaboration and if you like, future planning, looking at the best outcome for all generations in future times.

Enjoy this experience, expand your energies, link into those Atlantean memories and energies that will help develop your own awakening and progress and reconnection to All That Is, for you all are making progress and awakening at this glorious time on Earth.

Express your appreciation, your amazement, your love and understanding of the wholeness of All That Is, and be glad to be part of it as we are glad to be working with you, and sharing your development as our dear Atlantean Crystal Master, our emissary on the earthly plane. We will be with you today, as always; tune into our love, dear one, all will be well, and all is well.

We thank all those who are finding their own place in which to celebrate 12-12-12 and 21-12-12 and enjoy your part in all of this, for all those who are awakening and being part of this wonderful time, and to all those yet to awaken to the glory of All That Is, we send our greatest love, honour and respect and await with anticipation the outcome of these two amazing events in the life cycle of the human race and your beautiful planet Mother Earth."

Celebrating 12-12-12

What a magnificent experience.

As we approached Avebury, the frost glistened on the trees and the grass in a thick coating of sparkly whiteness.

Many people were already out enjoying the energies and celebrating the special day, groups were meditating; others were walking, chatting, playing music, chanting and glorying in the clear bright energies.

Needing to find a quieter space, I headed off to an avenue of stones in a separate area and walked up the hill between the stones. At the rise of the hill, the countryside opened out into gently rolling hills, it seemed that they provided a circle of protection around the stone circle, and with the frost highlighted the contours of the land, it was a magical scene.

exhilaration and celebration

As I walked up the hill, I sensed the beautiful, deep blue/purple energies of Archangel Michael guiding me and felt his strength and power. I paused at the top of the hill, and felt such exhilaration and celebration at the events occurring around the world, and felt a strong connection to the ancient wisdom and knowledge contained within the energies of the stones.

Archangel Michael stayed with me, and as I walked down the hill, I was drawn to touch some of the massive stones; my favourite one resembled an angel's wing. Other people had gathered at the end of the avenue of stones and were dancing and playing, as I approached, they all dispersed, allowing me to enjoy the energies in peace and solitude.

appreciation and amazement

I recalled the suggestion of The Crystal Team to "invite the energies to open, flow, connect, link and spread out in the most glorious way, forming those predetermined connections, forming those grids and securing in the light and the love, the appreciation, gratitude, love, honour and respect that has been awaiting these moments in their history, to awaken now at this time in a joyful, harmonious, symmetry of light and love. Express your appreciation, your amazement, your love and understanding of the wholeness of All That Is and be glad to be part of it."

It was a glorious experience and I felt very privileged to be able to take part in this amazing occasion.

Unification of Energies

Avebury was only one place where celebrations were held, and I wondered about the other events around the world. I asked The Crystal Team about the success of the universal events occurring on 12-12-12 and their impact on the 144 Crystalline Grid.

****

"Oh dear ones, the events of yesterday's time period over the universal time-span were magnificent, wonderful, amazing and beyond all expectations. As people around the world linked in to the energies creating the crystallisation of the 144 crystalline grid then the skies lit up and magic happened for you all.

nothing happens by chance

You see, dear ones, over a period of time, events and energies have been laid down in parts that were in preparation, or readiness, if you like, for these major times and opportunities, and on these special occasions energies enter your orbit allowing for the unity and connection of the parts to create a whole.

Stonehenge and Avebury were two locations within your area that were pivotal in the unification of energies for this completion and as you noticed they are in alignment and are of similar energy names of Amesbury and Avebury.

And again, as with the energy of names of individuals (read more about this in 'The Energy of Your Name' later in this book), so too the energy of place names applies here, so these two similar sounding places near ancient stone circles hold a similar energy within the context of the purpose for their creation – for as you will see, nothing is by chance and nothing happens without a reason or a purpose.

So linking the energies of the stones, the names, the alignment of the stones and further sets of stones around the world, this creates the alignment of energy and purpose with All That Is, for all time, on all levels and in all dimensions.

communication systems

The crop circles which abound in the area – although not all are genuine – are also part of this communication system within the outer reaches for it is not only humanity on Earth which benefits from the alignment, but alignment visible from the outer reaches of space is also crucial to the bigger picture, and so as all things link up on all levels they come together in a massive energetic structure or grid which holds the energy and intention of all that is being made available to you on all levels, and all dimensions.

And so, dear ones, do you see that not all knowledge and awareness is made available to you until the timing is at the most optimum for all the pieces of the jigsaw to fall into place in a way that your conscious minds can understand, accept and comprehend that these events and 'things' are for your benefit, and for the benefit of all mankind, all living beings, and all the universe and beyond?

And so we see the alignment, or the confirmation and setting of the grid in all its glory and know that this is the bedrock for the next major event on 21-12-12 which will be an even bigger cause for celebration on Earth.

guidance from Archangel Michael

For yourself, dear Lindsay, dear Atlantean Crystal Master, your part in linking into the Atlantean energies, in linking into the crystal energies within the Earth was a source of great light and love, as the lights, energies, wisdom and knowledge within the crystals awakens and are activated and as the energies spread in the colours of light that you saw, and unite around your planet, they spread out rays of light, love, compassion, wisdom, understanding and grace for the benefit of all.

It was important that you found the solitude in which to do this and were guided by Archangel Michael who worked with your energies uniting and igniting all these aspects on a grand scale.

The light at Avebury, the people, the goodwill, the good intention, the reconnections, the meaningful presence of all these people on that special day was of great benefit, and we thank all those who were present in a physical sense or in a spiritual sense.

The connections made on many levels with people as they chanted, sang, danced, spoke or just enjoyed the energies present at Avebury will reaffirm to you all, on many conscious and unconscious levels, all that you inherently know and understand, and we look forward to the next event on 21-12-12.

The Significance of 21-12-12

After the wonderful experience at Avebury, I was in expectation of another momentous occasion on 21-12-12, and as I prepared to visit Glastonbury, the Heart Chakra of the Planet, The Crystal Team offered the following inspiring words.

****

"Oh, dear ones, with joyful delight we see the arrival of this special day on Earth, the day that has been talked about for so long.

The energies of the numbers of this day and the energies of intention set for this day in accordance with the Divine Plan in the same way that your names and place names hold the energy and intention of your purpose, so too do numbers, and the significance of the two special dates of 12-12-12 and 21-12-12 hold energies and intentions for major events in your earthly plane.

And as these energies become a reality, as the intentions of the purpose become a reality, then this brings in the most amazing light and love for you all. The wisdom and knowledge stored within the Atlantean crystal skulls enabling the Mayan people, as you called them, to create the Mayan Calendar, was designed to end at this time to coincide with the In Breath and Out Breath exchange signifying a change in the Earth's energies, and so it all ties in together that as one period ends, as the breath of life and God changes, so too the energies of life on Earth change, and all this works together in a glorious way.

For you see, dear ones, nothing happens by chance and everything has a purpose, so all things are planned and all things work together in harmony, all things need to be laid down and prepared in order for these massive changes to occur on a global scale.

welcome in the new energies

And so, as you celebrate this special day, welcome in the new energies, welcome the wonderful changes that are being bought about and relish in the start of the new era, the new Golden Age.

A ceremony in some part of Glastonbury would be a very fitting way to mark this starting; this new beginning, of the new age. For where better to be than at the very heart of all things, the very heart centre where love emanates and abides, from the very energies of love, companionship, unity, joy, happiness and all the other words, feelings, essences and senses that make up this very special world.

the beginning of the new Golden Age

And so, to be at the very heart, at the centre where the Heart Chakra evolves, radiates, pulsates, if you will, the very centre of the cosmic heart linking you to the universal heart and thus to Source, how wonderful to be there on the occasion of the start of the beginning of the new great Golden Age.

And so, to spread your golden footsteps at the start of the beginning of the Golden Age, to link your energies through your Earth Star Chakra to those of the Heart Chakra, to merge and blend, to give and receive, to become as one with All That Is in this cosmic moment in time will be of great significance to you all, and to Mother Earth for, with all living beings, she can sense the good intent, the positive energies of those who walk upon her crust, and so she too will benefit from this golden energy.

And as you walk, and focus on this wonderful event to mark a change in times, focus on your love and intention for yourself, for Mother Earth, and for All That Is, seen and unseen, understood and not understood, known and unknown and enjoy and relish your part in the magnificence and glory.

Dear Lindsay, dear Atlantean Crystal Master, wonder around Glastonbury, visit the Chalice Well Gardens, find some quiet spots to link into the energies of the heart centre, consecrate the energies from Avebury, The Hurlers, crystals around the world, the crystalline grid, the crystal skull grid, link your Atlantean energies to all of these energies.

celebrate this special occasion

Celebrate this special occasion, walk with golden footsteps, see the Heart Chakra of the world expanding and igniting all the ancient wisdom and knowledge, see the connection to the other chakras and to the universal energies and bring in the love and light of God. And as you walk and focus on this wonderful event to mark a change in times, focus on your love and intention for yourself, for Mother Earth, and for All That Is, seen and unseen, understood and not understood, known and unknown, and enjoy and relish your part in the magnificence and glory. This will be a significant day for you all."

Celebrating 21-12-12

Glastonbury was bathed in glorious sunshine, and as we approached the town, we could see a procession of people already walking up the Tor. The town was busy with people heading for their chosen place of celebration and whereas Avebury had a sense of sacred silence, Glastonbury was alive with excitement.

In the Chalice Well Gardens I spotted a curved two-seater bench at the top of the garden and although I had imagined sitting alone for my meditation, it later occurred to me that the empty seat was made available for other people to sit awhile and make connections on higher levels.

As I sat and prepared to start my meditation, I felt the warmth of the sun on my face and heard the hum of excitement, celebration and joy as groups chanted, talked, and played music. The meditation itself was beautiful; I connected to the crystal in the centre of the Earth and linked to the crystalline grid and the crystal skull grid. I sensed the Heart Chakra of the planet open and resonate with glorious colours and the energies of love. I was aware of people joining me for a short while, before moving off to another part of the garden. As I came to the end of my meditation, gentle drumming started to resonate around the garden; it was as if the energies were being radiated out with the rhythm of the drum.

This was another truly exceptional day and a privilege to be part of.

Celebrations around the World on 21-12-12

The celebration in Glastonbury was only one of hundreds of events taking place around the world on this special day. I tried to imagine the effect of all these other celebrations around the world, creating wondrous energies of light and love; and asked The Crystal Team for their perspective of these events.

****

"Ah blessed ones, the events of the day in your timeframe of 21-12-12 were a stupendous occasion allowing in the light and love of God in even greater strength and capacity for you all.

As has been confirmed, the activation of the 144 Crystalline Grid allowed for the structure, the physicality, if you will, of the basis for the next stage of the Divine Plan to unfold in all its glory.

the bigger picture

For without a firm structure, the energy would be too strong to be contained within your orbit but as the grid was activated, the structure enables this additional light and love to flow into your orbit and into the universal field and out and out and beyond.

And so as we arrived at the glorious date of 21-12-12 with the anticipated events occurring around the world, the skies lit up with the good intentions, purpose, love and glory that welcomed in the new energies.

For without the goodwill of sufficient people on Earth to rise to the occasion, this would not have happened, for with Free Will, this cannot be enforced into the human realms. But this did happen, enough enlightened souls showed their commitment, their honesty, their love for Mother Earth and all living beings, and opened their hearts and minds to accept and welcome the new energies being made available to them.

help is available

And this allowed the energies to enter your earthly orbit and to be supported by the 144 crystalline grid put in place beforehand. And so, dear ones, all is now in place for the further unfolding of the Divine Plan, for the light and love of God in greater strength to be made available to you all. And as these elements are absorbed and integrated into your orbit, into your personal systems, then changes will begin to occur which will evidence to your conscious minds, that we are part of a bigger picture, that help is available to you all on a grander scale than you can possibly imagine yet, and all will unfold in all its magnificence.

The singing, chanting, drumming, the noise or general hubbub of chatter, excitement, happiness of all souls joined together in a common purpose that this day has arrived at last that this momentous day in the history of the universe, has arrived at last.

And the vibrations of the people on the Tor, in the streets, the Abbey, the Gardens, all generated wonderful connections, and these joined with the energies of all those other events, ceremonies, celebrations and so on around the world, creating the most wonderful and amazing connections, vibrations, light, intentions and commitments of service to a greater cause that welcomed in the new dawn, the new era, with such joy and happiness and joy.

making connections

And, dear ACM, for your part of solitude, peace, serenity and commitment, linking into the heart centre of the world, linking into the energies of the glorious crystal in the centre of the Earth, linking to the Atlantean and Lemurian energies, and bringing all that together with the energies of The Hurlers and Avebury made the most beautiful connections of power, wisdom, knowledge and light, and we salute and thank you for this work, it was magnificent.

And as you sat in the specially prepared seat for two souls, you made connections on many levels with those who came and sat by you and those who passed you by, for there were many connections made on that day in the wonderful energies, and these connections will be receiving the ancient wisdom and knowledge of Atlantis that you will receive on your holiday." (This refers to a holiday planned for January in the Canary Islands.)

"And as you are becoming aware, there are many ways of making connections other than verbal or even physical ones, as has been before and so will be again, as your conscious minds open and expand in the new energies. And these have been used before but have been closed down as life became more challenging for humans over different life stages but it enabled much to be achieved that is not understood in your current awareness.

So be open-minded on the power of connections and energetic fields, as this will be further revealed to you as you work more closely with the crystal world following your connections or should we say reconnection to the Atlantean crystal world, and as your connections and energies from many sources and aspects are growing in ways that you cannot yet see rest assured they are there, and we watch with joy and happiness as all this unfolds for you, the joy of being reconnected to your Atlantean energies, the joy of reconnecting to the wonderful crystal world of Atlantis. We send our greatest love, as always."

Blessings of Love

"Our love is expansive, eternal and universal across all times, levels and dimensions, and as such is available for you at all times in all circumstances and all situations.

Breathe in the love and light of God, feel it being absorbed into your beingness and place your trust in the universal process of life.

Blessed be to all souls at this time."

2013 - The Dawn of the New Era

"We wish you all great joy and happiness at the dawn of the new era, the new Golden Age, and await the changes planned for 2013 in your timeframe to develop and unfold.

As your awareness expands in the light and love of God, your conscious minds reconnect to all the ancient wisdom and knowledge now being made available to you all, and this will create great joy and happiness for you all.

As your auras expand exponentially, your perception and interpretation adapts to the new energies and you become aware of all that is being made available to you. And as this integrates into your consciousness, so your happiness quotient grows and glows, and lifts your spirits literally and physically, and so your heart centre expands and fills with the love and light of God, and as this light shines brighter, so it blends and links and unites as one, until all lights shine as one great star, as one great beacon of love and light. How magnificent is that?

As the water cleanses and clears all negative aspects from your earthly plane, as the storms and fires stir up energies to shift stagnant energies that are no longer relevant to this earthly plane of existence, so new brighter, lighter energies enter, and as some of you have already noticed, these energies are lighter, brighter, sharper, clearer and of a higher vibrational frequency; these energies are crystal-clear, dear ones, for now the 144 crystalline grid is fixed within the universe, then the effects add crystal-clear energies and a new level or dimension of experience for you all.

And these energies are more intense in their ability to communicate the light and love of God and the intention and purpose of clarity and harmony, and may take some adjustment for you all, as they are more powerful and effective than you have previously experienced on this earthy plane, although they are familiar to you on an unconscious level.

And so as you turn into the new year timeframe and integrate and absorb these energies, as Mother Earth clears all her energies, a dramatic shift will occur for you all, and this will continue to grow and develop over your timeframe, and we await with great anticipation as the Divine Plan unfolds for you all, in all its glory for you all.

With our greatest love."

Acting with Integrity

Introduction

Dictionary definition – honesty from Latin integritas = wholeness or purity

The subject of Integrity arose during one of our regular meditation groups. After our first meditation, we shared our insights and a discussion followed on acting with integrity during difficult situations. During the second meditation, one of our group began to channel a message for us all to assist our understanding and awareness.

We were given an image of what integrity could look and feel like so that we could have a reference point to measure our own sense and awareness by. The image focused on the heart centre and described a substance similar to a firm jelly with a heart in the centre. This substance was required to be absolutely round, smooth, whole and complete; this would indicate integrity of the highest order. Any glitches, roughness or out of shape elements would indicate that integrity was not complete.

We were delighted to receive this information and image and spent some time discussing our impressions and feelings about it. Further enlightenment on this subject is offered by The Crystal Team ...

"We were interested to hear the discussion on integrity between you all in your group and were delighted with the comments and image given through our dear Murray. The image presented at the heart centre was very specific and clear concerning the importance and clarity – not the best word for us to convey our information – of integrity. For integrity cannot be a half-hearted thing, it either is or it is not 'full of integrity'; there is no half measures and so the image was quite exact that the shape and feel should be strong and full and feel complete. For integrity, dear ones, comes from the heart centre, it is being integregous for yourself and the person or people who you are acting with or communicating with and in this sense, you cannot be sort of full of integrity, you either are full of integrity or you are not. We seem to stress this point, dear ones, for there are some occasions when it is enough to be nearly or partly there, but with integrity this is not the case.

Integrity – from integral – means of the whole, the complete whole and not part of the whole. And when you are dealing with matters of the heart and of communicating with other people on a level that encompasses so many aspects of love, intention and purpose, then you are required to be in the place 'of the whole'.

the bigger picture

Love is the energy of all things and that includes love for yourself, Mother Earth, all living beings and those aspects which are not yet apparent to you all, in the spiritual world. And so to act with integrity must come from a place that is good for you personally, not to underestimate or belittle your own place in this existence, your own power or your purpose. It also requires the same love for the person or people you are communicating with or the actions you are considering taking. And so the outcome must be centred on all the aspects for the good of all in the bigger picture.

We, and you, dear ones, understand that on a soul level, our soul essence is perfect; the beautiful connection to Source, the beautiful love and light energies that radiate from the soul centre is perfect and complete. On the earthly plane and with Free Will and distractions of the lower energies, some aspects of behaviour may be exhibited that are not necessarily in alignment with the love and light of the soul energy. And so in communications of all sorts, remembrance of that light and love of the soul energy of yourselves, dear ones, and those people or aspects that you are working with, will assist in maintaining the right purpose behind the words or actions. Seeing the bigger picture, being aware of these energies that we have discussed before, those light, bright, sparkly energies behind kind words, behind the words spoken behind a smile, of the positive range of energies from good intentions, and so these should also be taken into account when acting with integrity.

And so, dear ones, this automatically lifts your thought processes, your actions, deeds, intentions and words into the higher energies, out of the darker, lower, denser energies. And when your intentions come from this higher energy, this higher intention, then your heart centre grows, and glows and radiates out light and love and sparkly energies and then the solution arises out of these higher level energies because your intention has been of the highest purpose.

raising your energies

Imagine, dear ones, passing your 'issues' to this higher level, raising your awareness, your good intentions, and allowing the love and light and purity and clarity of your soul essence, your soul energy, your connection to Source, to dissolve, to release all those lower energies, to bring the situation into the light where it can be resolved with love and joy.

And then when your heart centre is filled with this love and joy, when your intentions have been of the highest, the image you received of the fullest integrity will be what you sense and feel and experience. And, dear ones, you can check out this feeling within yourself by sitting quietly, by concentrating on your heart centre, on this image, on the feelings within your body and your mind and your spirit, and when you feel light, bright, joyful, peaceful and the image is whole and complete and settled and joyful, then you know that all is well.

We thank you for the opportunity yesterday for this question to be raised and are delighted as always to transmit through our dear Lindsay, the words, intentions, information and energies to help you all to move forwards in your understanding, your awareness and conscious-minded development with ease, joy and harmony.

Our greatest love to you all."

The Crystal World

"Today, dear ones, our focus is to be on the beauty and power and magnificence and wonder of the crystal world. The light that emanates from them, the light and the love, the brightness, the joy, the creativity, the power and the glory of God, Source, or what you will, that emanates from the crystal world is such a joy to behold.

Imagine, dear ones, if you could see all aspects of this gift from God, all aspects of the frequencies, formations, the structures, the inner wisdom and inner knowing of these beautiful objects, then you would be overwhelmed by the magnificence. And within the crystal world, within these magnificent gifts, lie the secret, the wisdom, the knowledge and the link between the past, the present and the future.

crystals are magical record keepers

For as some of you now have the understanding of how crystals were formed, of the eons of time during which they came together in all their glory, the changes that occurred on your earthly plane during that time, of the changes of energies, the changes of landscapes, the changes of temperatures, all these alone would create a magical record keeper, holding the history, the story, the unfolding of the Divine Plan in all its glory.

And yet, added to this, is the light of God, the love, the compassion, the understanding, the desire for a happy life for all living beings within and upon the Earth, a desire for harmony, peace, love, joy and understanding.

Add to this already potent package, the different minerals and elements within the crystalline world that make each crystal so individual, colourful and potent for its own particular use. And again add to all this, the power of nature, the power of water within the ground, the power of the changing seasons, the shifts within the Earth plates, the changes and adaptations of Mother Earth herself.

And then add to all this the gifts that Mother Earth provides for the crystal world, the environment for them to grow and develop over eons of time, the environment of peace and safety, harmony and joy for them to develop to their fullness for, without the love and understanding of Mother Earth these things would not be possible. It is her agreement that allows all these things to take place on Earth, it is her agreement and consent that creates the environment for the crystal world, and allows it full development, variety and beauty.

So can you begin to see, dear ones, how wonderful this is, how amazing and powerful when all this comes together, when all aspects and facets of all these parts and components come together to create these beautiful objects?

And can you sense and feel the generosity of Mother Earth for her part in all of this, for her generosity and greatness to allow the creation of the crystal world within her being? And can you see the love of Source who created the opportunity for all of this to occur; the generosity, foresight, love, compassion, wisdom and understanding to arrange for the creation of these powerful gifts within the presence of Mother Earth?

linking to the very heartbeat of All That Is

For as all these aspects come together, so we are able to link into the energies of the crystals to reconnect to the love, light, compassion, understanding, joy, harmony and appreciation that lie within them. We can admire and display these beautiful, individual pieces of crystal and just focus on all that is contained within it, all the love and light that radiates out from it for the benefit of all. So, on a visual level we can appreciate its beauty and magnificence, and at the same time, enjoy the radiance of its light and love.

And then, we can sit and attune to this crystal and having absorbed its beauty and love and light, we can tune into the history and the glory that is contained within. And when you have an understanding of the glory and magnificence of what is contained within this crystal, so then you can absorb the energies and the glory of All That is. All the beautiful energies of Mother Earth, the beautiful energies of her generosity and consent, the beautiful energies of the compassion, love, light, wonder and awe at the formation of these wonderful crystals within Mother Earth. The amazing energies of the history of the Earth - and as the Earth does not exist in isolation – then so too do you absorb the energies of Mother Earth's connection to the universe, to the energies of the stars, the constellations, the galaxies and so on. And as you hold a piece of crystal in your hand you can begin to get a feel for all of these things.

And as your connection to the crystal develops, as your vibrations link to that of the crystal, as you absorb all of the history, the love, the generosity, the different components of the crystal, then so too are you linking to the very source of All That Is, to the very centre of All That Is, to the very heartbeat of All That Is.

And as your energy field reconnects with that which it already inherently knows and understands, as your conscious mind begins to shift its perception, and as your unconscious mind reconnects to the memories it holds, then your energy field will expand exponentially with greatness, love, joy, wisdom and gratitude and appreciation. Your cellular structure, your DNA will delight in the reconnection to these energies, to the reconnection to Source, to the fount of All That Is. And as this miracle occurs, so you will be able to release more of what does not serve you any longer, of what is not necessary for you to carry any more, and this can all be released with joy and blessings; release all that no longer serves who you are or who you wish to be as we move forwards into the new era, the new Golden Age.

we are now in this special time in the Earth's history

And dear ones, as you sit and admire or hold those crystals, express your appreciation and gratitude, for crystals are living beings and appreciation and love in return for this makes them shine even brighter and more gloriously.

Thank Mother Earth for her generosity, for, dear ones, nothing happens by chance and just as Mother Earth agreed to host humanity's existence in this timeframe, as she agreed to provide shelter, sustenance, water and a home for you all, these things do not happen by chance for they are all part of the unfolding of the Divine Plan, a Plan laid down for you all eons of time ago, and now we are in this special time in the Earth's history, a time of great change, great potential and great opportunity for you all. The opportunity created for you to experience a wonderful existence, one of joy and harmony, honour and respect, gratitude and appreciation for all living beings and Mother Earth.

Enjoy, dear ones, these God given gifts in all their magnitude and beauty, work with them for they are here to help you all, meditate with them, link into their wonderful energies, use your intuition in choosing them, talk to them, laugh with them and they will serve you well.

With our greatest love and appreciation."

Spreading the Light and Love

Starlite, my fluorite crystal skull, indicated that his energetic presence may soon be returning from whence he came as his purpose for being here is nearly complete. I wondered if he would like to communicate with us further before the time came for his energetic presence to depart from our orbit. We thank Starlite for sharing his wonderful wisdoms and for the work which has been undertaken for the good of all.

"Oh dear ones, it has been such a pleasure for me to be in the vicinity of your earthly plane for the time necessary to complete that which was my purpose in this timeframe.

Your earthly plane of existence is at such a pivotal point at the moment and so much love and light is being made available to you all.

It is our joy and delight to see the spreading of these beautiful energies and to know that the necessary links and connections have been made within the galactic grid as to ensure that the light and love are made available to all those in all far reaches of space and beyond.

The crystalline grid of which we speak is almost a technical structure that allows for advanced communication in all areas and reaches of space, and as you are aware, I have been concerned or concentrating on, not the best words here as they imply an element of hard work and this is not the case, but the structure is nearly finalised and settled and all the energies of love and light are now nearly available to all these planned areas at this time.

the bigger picture

And so, dear ones, delight in the availability of this love and light, know that within the sacred geometry of all things, that with all crystalline structures and grids and other awareness's, that the strength and loving intention and communication of these energies is immense, that it is strong and powerful yet gentle and kind.

For the love that emanates from God – or as some of you prefer, Manna – is so gentle, well intentioned, benevolent, eternal and powerful, it cannot but assist you all to raise your energies at this special time.

As more of you wake up to a bigger picture concept, that you are on a soul journey, that you are part of the whole, you will be able to access this energy more easily and more powerfully. As you raise your energies in line with the changing energies of all around, so you are not only helping other people to raise their energy awareness, but also to reboot, as you say, to add to the energy quotient within the grid, within the shapes, patterns, codes and so on which are within the bigger picture.

As you raise your energies, dear ones, those around you can only but be affected positively as they sense the change in your beingness, the soul essence which beams out love and joy and makes a connection with the structure and being of the soul essence of all other beings alive at this time.

access the beauty of nature

And how can that not then affect their conscious mind and awareness as they 'feel' happier, more joyful, access the beauty of nature, become more aware of all that Mother Earth and Mother Nature provide for you all?

And as this awareness increases, you will all become aware of the benefit of working in harmony with Mother Earth as you will naturally 'get it' and understand that it makes sense to work with her energies and respect her as a living being, as a part of the whole, as another being created by the Godhead to provide you with food, shelter, sustenance, and above all a place in which to experience this lifetime here and now.

For Mother Earth is a living being, her earth plates move and change, she has her energy centres, or chakras as does your human body. She has her life plan or agenda, if you wish to call it that, she has her own purpose within the whole universe and her own true path and purpose.

Mother Earth and Mother Nature are words that naturally imply nurturing, providing, love, care, compassion, understanding and this is not only for all living beings who are given this opportunity, it is also for herself, for loving yourself is an important basis for this journey for all beings. You cannot truly love if you do not love yourself.

And so Mother Earth must love and protect herself and when harm is done to her by ignorance, greed, carelessness and other unloving actions, then she must take action to protect herself for her own beinginess, protect her existence as part of the whole bigger picture, protect herself to be able to undertake her part, her role, if you like, within the bigger picture.

working in partnership

And so do you see how it needs be that all living beings respect, honour, love and appreciate all that is provided for them, and all that is available to them, and how working together in harmony with Mother Earth, honouring and respecting her needs, purpose, true path and all aspects of her beingness along with all that she can provide for your humanity – what a partnership is that, dear ones?

We use the word partnership deliberately to remind you of the wonderful atmosphere and energies created at the London Olympic Games (2012) where volunteers or Game Makers gave their time joyfully and lovingly and helped to create a wonderful experience for all.

How organisers worked in partnership with groups to get the job done on time to the best outcome for all. All groups athletes, media, medical support, transport; all aspects working together with the intended outcome of creating a wonderful spectacle for the benefit of all.

shine your light

So harmony, joy, partnerships, all create this wonderment and this can be yours again, dear ones, as you all wake up and continue on your journey of enlightenment and discovery.

Enjoy this journey; enjoy each new discovery and 'light bulb' moment, as you say, each step that brings you nearer to your real essence, to your true path and purpose, to your real and true perfect self. Share, laugh, chat, enjoy and grow together in love, appreciation, respect, honour and glory of all that is available to you, and we will watch with great delight the strengthening and powering of the grids, shapes, patterns, codes and all other aspects that ensure, create and support the spreading and availability of the maximum love and light energies that are created for the benefit of all.

Shine your light, dear ones, and grow and glow in your own glory and in the shared glory of All That Is.

With our greatest love."

144 Crystalline Grid

"Dear Lindsay, dear ACM, we have been hoping for an opportunity to communicate on this important subject for both your awareness, and that of others now awakening to their crystalline connections, Atlantean and Lemurian connections at this auspicious time in the Earth's history.

For as we have said, this year is an important one in the Divine Plan laid down for you all eons of time ago, and whilst we do not use time in the same manner and with the same meaning that occurs in the earthly plane, it is a useful means by which to communicate the arrival of events and stages within the Plan.

ancient grids of knowledge and wisdom

For as you know, crystals are communicators, they are like the most massive and complex computers that you can possibly imagine, and as such play a vital role in the unfolding of the Plan.

As you witnessed when you worked with The Hurlers (December 2011), the awakening of the crystal energies is an amazing event and spectacle to be part of and demonstrates the massive power and magnitude of the properties of crystals. And so as crystals around the world are awakening and reuniting with the wisdom and ancient knowledge, the stories, the energies, the connections stored within them, so these energies are linking up and reconnecting and forming the ancient grids of knowledge and wisdom throughout the world.

If you can imagine switching on all the computers in the world, all at the same time, and all linking into the same programme, your computer systems would be over-loaded and crash, but with crystal power, the uniting of the crystal energies around the world creates a wonderful, an amazing and spectacular sight for your earthly plane and out, out, out into the universe and beyond; the massive light has been switched on and all the energies are joined and connected. This joining and connecting creates a strengthening and empowering of a hundred, thousand, million times to the power of individual components, and as this light glows and grows and spreads and reconnects it brings back all the ancient wisdom, stories, love, honour, gratitude, respect, appreciation, collaboration, co-operation, all the love and light that is now becoming available to you all, will be connected up by this grid.

And the 144 number is an important statement of energies and sacred geometry and connections that will reaffirm and reunite and solidify all these energies.

For energy is what it is all about, and a crystalline grid of energies of the most glorious, bountiful love and light will be of such benefit to all humanity and all living beings, to Mother Earth and the universe and beyond.

And so the setting and reuniting of these components must happen before 21-12-12 can occur and although not so well known in the events of this year, it is the fore-runner to 21-12-12 and is of vital importance.

Living in Joy and Harmony

"As you are seeing, more and more people are awakening to their inherent wisdom and knowledge, they are part of this world, they are part of the earthly energies, they are part of the whole, and so as the Earth energies change, they cannot but be affected by the changes, and as they sense more and more people tuning in to the new energies, they too will be encouraged to open, receive, integrate and acknowledge these energies, and more and more attention will be focused on living joyfully and harmoniously than is given to financial gain and false glamour. And in this way, the emphasis of how life is lived will change, and peoples' priorities will change, and their thoughts and actions will be more centred on love and compassion and consideration and collaboration and peace.

the light of God

And in this way, health for all people will improve as they are living within their true soul energies, and they will not be at odds with this energy but at harmony with it, and as such will be more peaceful and happy and content, and at one with All That Is.

And as their priorities change and they become more peaceful, loving, aware and consciously open, then they will be an example to others, and their energy will shine and glow for the benefit of themselves and for Mother Earth, and so as shown to you in your meditation groups, the gifts you were given, the symbols of inner light can become radiant with light and love, radiant with the light and love of God, and as all lights shine out into the universal energies, so they will blend, and grow and spread until all lights become one, until all lights unite and link and combine in one glorious magnificent light, and within this light there can be no discord or disharmony for it is the light of God, the Great Provider, the Great Fount of All That Is.

love never ends

When the energies of love and good intention abound in your aura, in your atmosphere and in the hearts of all people, there is no space for harmful, hurtful thoughts and actions, for revenge and retaliation, for greed and power, for pain and fear.

The energies of love bring forth all healing, all dissolution of fear and anger, of lack of understanding and compassion, of lack of being loved and being loveable, for when love abounds, you are at one with the very heart of All That Is, at the very heart of what God intends for you all, at the very heart of love itself and this is the greatest gift to you all, and is being made available to you all, as we move into the new era, the new Golden Age.

And so, dear ones, we leave you with the thought, the intention, the energy of love, wrap yourself in it, breathe it in, see it enfolding you and entering every cell in your body and know that there is an inexhaustible supply of love, for love never ends.

And this love will unite you all in the most glorious energies of magnificence beyond your current awareness, but this can be yours, dear ones, it can be yours, and these events are another vital part of the process of achieving this

wonderful, magnificent life on Earth within the wonders of the universe and beyond.
With our greatest love."

Laughter – a priceless gift!

"A Day without Laughter is a Day Wasted." - Charlie Chaplin

Laughter is such a gift and it is free, fun, readily available and best shared with others. We all know we feel better for a good laugh - here are a few of the reasons why -

- Laughing strengthens the immune system
- It boosts energy
- Relaxes muscles
- Diminishes pain
- Protects the heart by improving the function of the blood vessels and increasing blood flow – this helps protect against cardiovascular problems
- Defuses conflicts
- By altering our perspective, it helps us maintain a positive outlook on life
- Laughing triggers endorphins which make us feel better
- It strengthens relationships adding vitality, freshness and resilience
- It unites people in a unique way, bringing shared joy and happiness

The Crystal Team offer - "Laughter, dear ones, is indeed the best medicine for the reasons described above, and on an energetic level its beneficial effects are magnified.

When you laugh you raise your energies to a new level of joy and happiness and when you share this with others the level of joy and happiness increases immensely; not only do you gain individually and then as a group, but also you gain by shining your light clearer and brighter for all others, and the group energies extend into the universal energies to clear and cleanse and to lighten and brighten all around.

So if you can imagine the lovely sparkly energy around yourself, magnify this many times with those you share your laughter with and then see this light, bright energy spreading out into the universal energies and out and out further and further. So in effect the more you laugh the more you are clearing and cleansing your own energetic field and that of all around you.

So we encourage you to laugh, and we celebrate all laughter of all people, of all races, cultures and ages around the world; laughter is a gift indeed, dear ones, and you are invited to use, share and enjoy this gift as often and frequently as you can.

Delight in the laughter of babies, the innocence and laughter of young children as they discover the world around them, delight in your jokes, your sense of humour, your ability to see the funny side of things and this will help you to raise your energies in line with the changing energies of Mother Earth, and this alignment will be another factor in assisting you to move forward into the new era with ease joy and harmony.

The gift of laughter is a blessed gift indeed, on all levels, across all times, and all dimensions; another of God's gracious gifts to you all, dear ones. Enjoy this gift of lightness and brightness and give thanks for this aspect of your lives.

Blessed be, dear ones, blessed be."

Peace on Earth

"Peace in your lifetime is achievable, dear ones, as you all raise your own awareness, as you begin to understand that peace comes from within before it can be without.

And by this we mean that without all the energetic imbalances that you have accumulated over this and many other lives, without the thoughts, deeds, actions, miscreations and resulting attachments, your heart centres will become pure, clear, loving, honest, and you will have clarity on all matters.

In this way you will be radiating pure love energies, and through this there can only be inner peace and sanctity and true alignment with your path and purpose in this lifetime.

Therefore inner work is of the greatest gift to yourself and all humanity, and must therefore be an individual quest for inner peace.

Your inner peaceful energies, your loving essence will then add to the growing energies of honesty, grace, sanctity and love, which are expanding exponentially on a global level.

Added to the energies as Mother Earth clears and cleanses her own energies allows for continued approachment to critical mass and a tipping point for all humanity.

This is the greatest service work you can undertake dear ones, and we applaud you all for your endeavours on this journey.

Outwardly working for peace without the internal clarity, awareness and clearance is not a sustainable option, although all endeavours of this sort are beneficial.

Combined on all levels with the intention of clearance and clarity, love and honesty will serve you all well dearly beloved ones, and we watch all your endeavours with great joy and appreciation.

This opportunity is open and available to you all on Earth dear ones, and we are here to help you in all ways, on all levels and across all dimensions.

So tune in, ask for help, be guided by the universal processes of life and above all have faith and trust, dear ones, faith and trust."

A Beautiful Meditation for Peace

"Take some deep breaths and make your connections with Mother Earth, allowing your energies to blend with hers knowing that you are working together to create joy, harmony, peace and clarity for all living beings at this time.

Breathe in the universal breath of life that connects all living beings, that connects you to the fount of All That Is that connects you to the creator of all your experiences and to the fount of all love.

Take in, absorb and integrate these gentle loving energies into every fibre of your being, see it enfold and engulf you in the loving energy of God, angels, archangels, beings of light, unicorns, rainbows, and all other light energies.

Feel the connection to the crystal beings whose manifestation into physical form was created by God for your benefit at this time, feel the connection of the crystal energies with Mother Earth and yourself as living beings.

See all things as part of the oneness, part of a common unity with yourselves as part of that beauty and glory.

Sense your inner being gently releasing all those aspects that do not fit with this image of love and oneness, all those hurts, sadness's, pain, disappointments, miscreations, words, deeds, thoughts that do not have a place within this image of love, joy and harmony, and see them gently floating to the surface to be released into the light, and gently dissolving and disappearing.

Feel the lightness within yourself, feel the relief at letting go of these redundant energies, and see yourself being filled with beautiful bright, sparkly, light, rainbow colours, angelic energies, unicorn loving essence, see yourself overflowing with the love energies of grace, sanctity, gratitude and joy. Breathe them into your aura, and see yourself as a spark of Divine love and light within the oneness of God's love.

remain in these energies for a while

Now see all people clearing and cleansing that which they are ready to release, see them filled with this amazingly bright, light, sparkly love.

See Mother Earth glowing in this light, see the rivers clear and pure, see the mountains radiating this light for miles around, see all living beings happy and joyful and safe and respected.

See the lights of all people joining, glowing, radiating and resonating as one, joined in unity, peace, harmony and joy.

See the change in energies creating peace on Earth, and see all people working together for the highest and greatest good of all.

Peace is achievable dear ones, Peace on Earth can be yours to experience and delight in, and peace starts with that sense of inner love, responsibility, awareness and intention.

We salute you all beloved ones, we salute you all, goodbye until time again"

Prayer for Peace
I pray for peace with all my heart
I pray for peace with all my mind
I pray for peace with all my soul

May peace reign supreme on Earth.

Spirits of Pure Love

Horses are spirits of pure love and willingness who offer to assist all souls who come into contact with them. They are also able to work in a very special way with children whose normal acceptable systems of communications are not as developed as in others, and this allows for the creation of a special relationship of trust and love.

"Horses, dear ones, are the most gentle and gracious of creatures who are on their chosen path in the existence that they have chosen in this lifetime on this earthly plane.

Their spirits are pure love and willingness to assist all those who come into contact with them. They are a strong link with the energies of Mother Earth as they live a very grounded, natural existence in the wild, and when working with human beings in a formal setting they are still very much connected to Mother Earth through the ground they walk on, the grass they eat and the very nature of their soul connection to nature and all living beings.

And so, in all their connections with humanity, they bring through this loving, nurturing, essence of connection to Mother Earth; to her compassion, understanding, to her desire to provide for you all, and to her protective nature.

unspoken communication

So bringing this love, compassion and sustaining energies through their spirit, adding this to their own energy of love, willingness to help and their ability to communicate on many unspoken levels with all people and all living beings, enables these noble spirits to assist all who allow these energies into their awareness.

The communication systems that exist in non-verbal levels enable horses to understand and work with those children and adults whose normal acceptable systems of communication are not as developed as in others. This allows horses to work in an intuitive level and allow the souls of the children to open and accept love and compassion, understanding and encouragement that they are unable to accept in normal communication systems.

trust and acceptance

The purity of the love, the connection to Mother Earth energies, allows a relationship of trust and acceptance to develop in the purest sense and allows new developments within the body to open up and create new forms of communication and to create a strong bond of affection and recognition on a soul level.

This mutually beneficial relationship between these two manifestations of energy forms, is a delight to see on many levels, and we congratulate and appreciate all those people who understand this on an instinctive level and who are able to provide special horses for special people and all those who provide the opportunity for souls to experience this wonderful love and communication on many levels.

The benefit to all concerned in the bigger picture of families, friends, and in many ways and many levels, is a wonderful sight, and so we thank you all and send love to you all and we are here for you to link into our energies at any time.

With our greatest love and appreciation."

Life in other Dimensions

There is much speculation about life in other dimensions. Is it possible that we are the only life form within this vast arena of space? Many people have recorded footage of unidentified flying objects, and controversy exists between official bodies and those who firmly believe in their existence. But even seeing an unidentified flying object does not give us any clues as to their identity or why they exist, so I asked The Crystal Team if it was appropriate, at this time, for us to learn more about them.

****

"As always, dear friend, we are happy to communicate with you for the benefit of yourself and other people, and it can be strange seeming for us to inform you of things which we know you know already, and have experienced before but have yet to reach in your earthly understanding.

Your inherent belief that these so called UFO's are true, is of course, correct. To think that life can only exist in one form in the great size of the universe and beyond is a very limited viewpoint, and one that is not correct.

As part of our soul growth we have chosen to experience life on Earth, on the earthly plane, in the physical form which works for humanity. As said before, the contract with Mother Earth to allow for humanity to exist, relies on many factors and all things working together; the need for humanity to have food, shelter, warmth, crystals, all these things are created as part of the package as you may say.

manifestations of energy

If life is chosen in another dimension then the form created for that existence would of necessity be compatible to the environment in which they were experiencing that particular part of their journey – that part of their soul essence and growth.

And as we know, energy can manifest in any form it chooses at any time and there are many forms of energy manifestation that are not yet within your understanding or awareness on a conscious level.

And so your scientists agree that it is likely that life exists in other forms within the universe but as yet cannot imagine what these forms would manifest like. And so as each stage of life in all levels and on all dimensions exists compatibly within the energy of love, we are all part of one and part of the same, and so these beings as you call them – these alien beings – are also a part of us, for in the bigger picture we are all part of the same, part of the whole, we are all one.

These objects as you call them are manifestations of energy within an advanced technological remit which have many purposes both for themselves and for humanity, and so one simple answer cannot answer all queries.

These forms, beings, energy manifestations are on their soul journey too, and as with your humanity you have light workers, peace workers, joy workers, Mother Earth workers and so on. Similarly these forms also have many varied purposes and aspirations; some of them may be involved with bringing knowledge and wisdom to Earth, some may be involved with their own enlightenment, some may be involved with education for their 'humanity', some may be explorative in the same way you send space craft to the Moon and Mars and have your satellite robots which fill the sky with energy manifestations for the benefit of your humanity.

celebrate life on Earth

So you can see dear ones that they are really no different from the experiences you are currently having on Earth and are beginning to have in the sky, in space, with the increasing awareness and knowledge you are gaining on space travel and the solar system.

And as your telescopes become more advanced and more of the space arena is revealed to you all, so your understanding and awareness grows on all levels and literally in all dimensions. For, as at one time your earthly settlers could not see or comprehend the existence of land and people on other continents, and their means of travel was slow and unsafe, so you are beginning a journey of exploring the space around your home environment in a different way.

This is being repeated in other dimensions and other existences within the Cosmos and as all aspects are brought together in one arena, in one big picture, so you see once again the connections with All That Is and with all that can be, and that more is revealed to you as you progress on your journey. And we would add that all things are perceived individually in very different ways by each and every one of you – determined by your life experiences, past and present, your personality, your purpose for this existence and your intuition and inner knowing, so no two experiences will be the same.

So we hope this has revealed a little more for you all on this question, and of course more can and will be revealed to you as you develop in awareness and understanding.

So celebrate all that is available to you, celebrate life on your chosen planet for this life experience, celebrate your true path and purpose in this lifetime and celebrate the love of God which has created all things and made all things possible.

Our greatest love to you all."

Clearing your Energetic Imbalances

"As we breathe in the same air as the trees and plants, animals and all wildlife, all living beings and Mother Earth, how can we be separate from them and not part of them?

As our auras expand in the love and light of God, how can we not but affect positively the energy that is around us and around other people?

How can we imagine that what we do or say does not impact on all that is around us? As the trees expire their energy and clear the air for us, how can that be separate from our energy, so if people are still carrying their energetic imbalances with them, then this must affect the energy of their aura and the energy they share with the world around them.

You cannot yet see the air as we do, but if you could you would see the effect of negative changes in your auras and how this spreads into the air around you, and this is taken in by all living beings as a form of pollution added to the chemical pollution that is in the air from the way of life which is sustained on Earth.

open your heart centres

And so , dear ones, your first responsibility is to clear your own energetic imbalances, open your heart centres and release all that no longer serves you, imagine your hearts glowing with love and light and allow this to shine out for all to see and experience, and in this way you will have a massive affect on all around you, for the birds, the trees, the flowers, the soil, all those things and aspects of life which seem separate and individual and nothing to do with you.

So see how this can change so quickly, see how immediately you can alter your thoughts, deeds, actions, intentions, hopes, dreams and aspirations to be focused in love, to be focused in the oneness of All That Is, linking into the love of God, the provider of all your experiences.

Life in a physical form is not always easy dear ones, and yet you have the manifestation that you have chosen; an opportunity for spiritual growth within the earthly plane and so enjoy all these other manifestations of energy as part of yourself.

magical happenings

See the beauty in the trees, the plants, the water, marvel at the variety, the sights, the sounds that are all part of you as you are part of them, connect your energies to the love and light of God and know that you are part of the whole, that you are part of the magic that is happening at this time on Earth as you all become aware of the bigger picture, aware of the love that is available to you, of the potential magnificence that awaits you as you move truly into your gloriousness within the love and light of God.

Look up to the stars, the moon, and the sun, to the universal energies, and know that you are part of the magnificence of All That Is and enjoy the energies of all that has been provided for you; it is truly magnificent when you enter your heart energies and connect to the love that is available to you, dear ones, a gift beyond measure indeed.

With our greatest love as always, till time again."

The Energy of Your Name

"Ah dear ones, this is a very lovely subject to be communicating with you, for names are a form of communication in themselves.

The names we chose to be given before we manifest on Earth are given much consideration and thought before they become reality on Earth.

The meaning, intention and energy of names is very important as this 'word' will be used many times on Earth, it will be written, spoken and communicated many times, and so the energies and intentions must be a good match with the energies of the person too.

The energy of the name will need to match the physical person for their entire life span on Earth although some of you do decide to change your official name, or use a shortened version of your name.

name energies change over time

Many of you as children adopt another name or are given another name by family or friends, and this may suit or fit for a stage in your life, but your name energies are really the most appropriate for you as an adult because the energies of the name match the energies of your physical body, and so create confirmation and unity between energies and existence and what you chose to experience here on Earth.

So can you see how an alteration in your name as an adult may create a mismatch between your name energies and your physical being? And so we would invite and encourage all people to use the name they chose to manifest in this lifetime; although as with all things you have Free Will and this will be your choice at this time.

And as the energies of your existence change, as Mother Earth changes, as the energies of the universe change, so the energy of names changes too, and so over many years the choice of energies of names alters and the intention and purpose of the name energies changes too and thus some names become less popular and new name energies emerge, and this pattern continues to change over the centuries.

like your name

The consideration of name energies takes many things into consideration as it allows the physical being and the subconscious mind to grow into the energies of the word, and so many people do not appear to like their name until they become at one with the intention and energies of their chosen name, and then they accept and like their name for it fits who they truly are and who they wish to be, and being at one with your name is a good indication of being at one with yourself, being at peace with your life, being in a place on your journey where on many levels you understand where you are, and where you are going.

And much information has been given and written about the meaning and purpose of the energies of names, and where this is accurately interpreted and honestly written, the meanings give guidance, understanding and encouragement of who you truly are and why you chose that name, and can help on conscious and unconscious levels to match your physical body energy to your name energy, thus helping you unite and be at one on all levels, and this can be reassuring in many ways.

And so for new parents, the name that manifests is the one that that physical being has chosen, and this is true in most cases, as is the fact that souls do chose their parents for the life learning they wish to experience although sometimes this may not be a match with what they actually experience in reality.

a gift from God

But again, we offer that the name energy stays with you always, that will always be the name, the energy you have chosen whether you use the name or not, so the energy intentions will always remain with you for you to tune into if you wish, and writing your name, meditating on it, speaking it even, will help you regain the alignment of energy purpose and intention and your physical being within this existence.

It is another example for you dear ones, of how many signs and how much help is available to you all on so many levels, seen and not seen, understood and not understood, and on all levels, so enjoy your name, for you were involved in the decision to choose these energies. Understand the deeper significance of your name and honour your name and honour the names of others.

It is all part of the Divine Plan, the divinity, the love, understanding and grace that is available to you all.

And so smile about your name, it really is a very significant part of who you are and why you are here, and see it as a gift from God who loves you all, and names each and every one of you as individuals and yet as part of the whole.

Smile when you say your name and other peoples' names, for we know that the energy behind that smile enhances all the intentions and energies, and be in alignment with who you are and with the universal energies of love. Till time again."

Blessing
I now resonate with All That Is, across all times, levels and dimensions,
world without end. Amen."

A Gift from God Indeed
An Elestial Crystal communication

Little specks of golden light shining from within
linking us to the light of God, working from within.
All the knowledge stored inside ready for release,
all the history of mankind held and stored for time.

Folded, coded, ready for the day when humanity is ready
to hear what it has to say.
Races, cultures past and present, stories and folklore,
held within this precious gift, a gift from God indeed.

And when the day at last arrives for cells to open out
to release all that is stored inside will be a day to shout
about the love of God that shines out bright

from the golden rays inside
that links us all in glorious ways, heart, by heart, by heart.

And information, tales and facts will be revealed at last
to help you all on Earth to move forwards very fast
into the love and light of God, these golden strands and rays of light
that link us all by day and night heart, by heart, by heart.

Bringing In the Feminine Energies

The Moon, dear ones, at this special time in the evolution of your existence on this planet in this dimension, is shining brightly to bring in the feminine energies of gentleness, understanding, love, compassion and peace.

Take in and absorb the beautiful gracious energies being offered to you. Allow them to integrate into your systems and be absorbed by your cellular structure, your DNA and your crystalline grid.

Allow these soft, bright, light, vibrant energies to show you the way forward into the new era which is approaching as we progress through this special time, and enjoy and be grateful for all that is being made available to you.

The position of the planets at this time, clearly indicating change and progress are confirmation of the changes that are occurring on all levels, and in all dimensions.

Celebrate the opportunity for personal growth, inner knowing and wisdom and share your joy and delight in all that is occurring at this time.

It is a most exciting time for you all, dear ones, for your dimension, the universe and beyond.

We send our greatest love to you all."

Messengers from the Angelic Realms

We all delight in seeing birds of all sizes, shapes and colours soaring high over the countryside and coming into our gardens eating newly dug worms or feeding from special feeders. The joy of hearing their delightful songs, especially when they herald the start of springtime, brings great pleasure to many.

During a meditation, whilst holding a white feather, I became more aware of the complexity of each feather, and how it is formed so uniquely to fit perfectly as part of the whole. The size, shape, weight, colour, all purposefully designed and created to allow the birds to fly, catch food, survive, sing and fulfil their purpose in their chosen existence.

I was keen to learn more and was guided to ask The Crystal Team for further information; and here is their beautiful reply.

****

"Birds, dear ones, as you well know, come in all shapes, sizes, types and colours and this variety is part of their charm and their survival.

For as you witnessed with the white feather meditation, and other insights into the magical way that the feathers are formed and created to come together in perfection and glory, so too is the variety of birds designed to assist in the role of Mother Nature, in the survival and expansion of forms of life on Earth. For as is always the case, life forms are continuously evolving and changing, and birds are excellent at adapting to their surroundings, and are also working in harmony with Mother Nature.

restoring harmony

Your awareness allows you to understand the important role that bees play in the propagation of plants, in the creation of honey, and in many other unseen ways. Experiments and tests allow you to understand their movements and dances and communications, and like many other species, they are affected by the negative energies experienced around your orbit at this time, and have suffered many diseases and problems within the bee community, or common unity systems.

It is expected that as the Earth's energies are cleared, following the clearance through flooding, fires, storms and so on, as the clearance removes stagnant energies that no longer have a place in the new dawn of ages, then clearer air, brighter, fresher air will allow for the bee communities to rebalance their energies and restore harmony and good health within their being, and as this happens they will become wholesome and joyful and will regain their sanctity and purpose here on the earthly plane.

And as with birds too, they are affected by the negativity, by the stagnant energies, as this has caused a disruption in their well-being and expected life-cycle of their communities, and again, the new energies of the new dawn, the new era, should allow for restoration of balance, health and harmony.

God's joy and love

So birds, dear ones, are your link to the heavenly realms, as they soar high into the skies, as they move and float and hover and dip and dive, they are creating wondrous energies and movement and connections with the heavenly realms.

It is no coincidence that angels are said to have wings to fly, for birds are angels' messengers; they are the connecting force between the realms spreading joy and happiness wherever they are.

And again it is no coincidence that white feathers are signs of angels calling and being in your presence, in your orbit, for they are the representation, the union of the heavenly realms being bought to you by their messengers, by their heavenly link, the birds.

So as you see the birds flying and soaring, think of them as angelic messengers, connections between the heavenly realms, uniting Heaven and Earth in all its glory.

As angel messengers on Earth, they are here to do a job as part of their remit for their existence, a joyful task and part of the laws of nature, part of the bigger picture and part of God's joy and love for you all.

For as they bring such joy in their songs, as they herald the dawn of the new day, and a new beginning of new opportunities created for you, so they lift your hearts and spirits joyfully and lovingly. So as you listen to the dawn chorus, be grateful for their part in welcoming in the new day, bringing the love of God, the light of God and the angelic energies for you all. Their range of sounds, their tuneful songs, their joy and happiness is created especially for all humanity, and all living beings, and for Mother Earth as part of the continuing love and light of God for your all.

your true path

The vibrational frequency of the range of sounds lightens the energies, and this raises the frequencies for all around, and then for their joy of working with Mother Nature to keep the balance by eating the grubs and insects, to maintain the order and flow of life on Earth. And these birds that migrate and take their songs, their joy, their energies, to pastures new for another season, so that they may maintain the balance of nature in these areas too.

And how the young birds are able to fly so soon after hatching, how these amazing gifts of God know where and when to fly to these new areas, how they know what is required of them, is stored in their internal systems, in their unconscious minds and is then brought to their consciousness when required.

In the same way, dear ones that your past awareness, your true path and purpose in this life-time, and your true soul essence, your Atlantean core essences, your ancient wisdom and knowledge, is all stored within your systems ready to be awakened at the appropriate time. For many of you this has already happened, and for many of you this time is now approaching, as the energies have been raised to a level sufficiently high to make those connections, to bring forth all those components within your DNA, cellular structure and crystalline grid, that have been stored there for this very time.

And so, dear ones, when you see the birds flying freely and soaring and gracefully moving through the skies, make those connections with the heavenly realms that created these wonderful gifts for you all. Feel yourself rising high in the skies, see yourself soaring and flowing with the angelic energies, see these connections between Heaven and Earth, feel yourself as part of that connection, that you can develop and strengthen that connection with the realms of Heaven and Earth.

you are not alone

See yourself as part of nature, as part of the whole picture, as part of the wonderful cycle of life and birth and rebirth, and as seeds are spread each year for growth and are then harvested, or continue to grow, and this is repeated continuously as the wonder of nature maintains a balance for all life forms on Earth. And how wonderful that Mother Earth accepted all these forms of life, all cycles of nature to grow, to feed all living beings, and provide all elements that are required, to enable all living beings to thrive and prosper on this planet, in this experiment, in this life-time.

Relish your part in this, as you are a part of the whole and not a unity of one, but part of the common unity, part of everything, part of the whole.

Relish the variety of wildlife that exists to maintain life on Earth, the delicate balance of food provided for all living beings and the cycle of propagation and seed dispersal played within this cycle. You are not alone and cannot exist alone, but working in harmony with All That Is, working as part of a community of common purpose enables all living beings to live in harmony with All That Is, with Mother Earth, and with all natural life forms within the universe whatever form they take.

gifts for all

And as the energies change, dear ones, as the energies raise, as your awareness raises, as your conscious minds reconnect to all you inherently know to be true, you will naturally come to understand the role of all things in maintaining the balance in all things, and you will naturally start to appreciate, value, and be grateful for, all that is being made available to you.

Your love and joy and sanctity in all things will increase many-fold, and this will bring you greater gifts than you can image as you see colours more clearly, as you feel the energies more beautifully, as your soul sings with joy at reconnecting to all the gifts laid down for you.

So as more is revealed to you, as you see more colours and more of what you cannot yet see, your joy and love and appreciation will increase, more than you can imagine, and the balance in all things will be restored.

And so with our greatest love and anticipation for the unfolding events, goodbye until time again."

The Tree Kingdom

"Standing tall, standing strong, this is the part we play in the world, sending our roots deep into the ground and our leaves and branches reaching up to the sky, a link between the Heavens and the Earth.

Our branches reach out in balance and harmony, spreading energies in all directions, providing shelter and habitation for living beings and plants.

Our roots stretch deep into Mother Earth, anchoring our energies, solidly and safely within the ground.

Our ancient wisdoms and knowledge are passed down through all generations and adaptations of our form.

We breathe in the air and digest and cleanse these properties and safely release them to the skies.

We help to heal the planet; we help to heal the Earth.

We are here to help you all, dear ones, to help you all.

Enjoy our beauty, respect our purpose, see us as living beings with a purpose just like your humankind.

We can work together dear ones, to keep our beautiful planet alive, healthy, joyful and balanced.

We are all part of the whole; we are all part of God's creation, equal in his light and love.

Our variety and purpose, our joy and delight in our existence is no less for being in our present form dear ones, we are all part of God's magnificent creation, part of the Divine Plan, part of the Oneness, and the unity of All That Is.

We co-exist in the magnificence of God's love for us all, we co-exist with the energy and the love that Mother Earth has for us all in allowing us this existence.

Together we are part of this whole magnificence, enjoy all our species, our energy manifestations, our fruits and our ancient wisdoms, respect our beingness, and our rite of passage as we respect yours, and marvel in the gloriousness of All That Is dear ones, for we are all creations of God's magnificent bounty and graciousness.

Blessed be to you all on this earthly plane as one magnificent being of light and love. Amen."

Music

"Listening to music, dear ones, is allowing your being to be moved by resonance, vibration and joy. When you tune into a piece of music that you enjoy, you are allowing the sounds to vibrate in harmony with your energetic field, with your soul essence, and with your mental processes.

For the music you choose will be fitting to the mood of your mentality at the time, so when you need a lift you will choose music that will lift your brain patterns, your energy and your overall beingness.

When you require relaxation, you will choose soothing patterns for the brain to tune into, for as we have said before, all is energy, all is part of one, and we are always trying to maintain that balance, that harmony within our beingness that keeps us in a state of well-being, joy and harmony. And music, working on a vibrational level is an excellent way of doing this.

Some sounds are discordant, and may aggravate your beingness, and may be a statement of imbalance, and again this is representative of your mental energy and resonance.

music evokes emotional healing

Music can evoke emotional healing too on many levels, and is a good medium for use in healing treatments as it absorbs the energy, and balances and harmonises the healing process.

Enjoy your chosen music, dear ones, and delight in the images and emotions it invokes, and give thanks for all the gifts that are available in whatever form they are packaged and presented to you.

Enjoy the beauty of the bird song, some of which is pitched at a very harmonious level for your humanity. Enjoy the music from the sounds of nature, the babbling brook as it rushes downstream, bouncing and bubbling over rocks and stones, enjoy also the silence of nature, the quietude, the peace and solace to be had in nature, for that in itself is a resonance and vibration to be enjoyed and to bring peace and harmony to your beingness.

Through the silence and peace you are strengthening your connection to all the beauty that surrounds you, all the gifts of Mother Earth, the beauty of all things natural, and so are strengthening your connection to Source who made all this possible dear ones, for you to experience in this lifetime, in this existence at this exciting time on Earth.

Enjoy the energy of the silence; enjoy the peace that comes with silence as part of all the gifts available to you.

With our greatest love."

Trees – the Lungs of the Planet

In 2012 it was recorded that Ash trees were showing signs of dis-ease and many had to be cut down. I asked The Crystal Team if they wished to comment on this distressing news. Here is their insightful reply.

★★★★★★★★★★

"These Ash trees of which you speak are one of nature's treasures that are showing signs of the stress and distress that is apparent in the imbalance within the laws of nature and Mother Earth.

As mentioned before, trees are the lungs of the planet and when the lungs cannot breathe easily in your human form – they become clogged up and cannot function effectively, and so manifest signs of dis-ease or illness.

In your human form these are treated with medication which, whilst alleviating the symptoms, does not relieve the cause of the illness, and so this still manifests in a physical way. In addition, the condition may be exacerbated by emotional considerations when a person is not fully at ease with the life conditions in which they live.

So, dear ones, you know in your humanity that problems with receiving enough oxygen into your blood-stream, allowing this to flow through your systems, through your heart, through your very core being, is being affected by these conditions on all levels, and so too with these beautiful trees, where the air is polluted, where the nutrients coming through the soil from the connections with Mother Earth, where the conditions are not good for these trees to thrive and prosper and breathe and grow, then they too will exhibit signs of dis-ease.

The symptoms have been developing for some time before the manifestation of this condition which is now being perceived by your experts, and we send our greatest love to the soul energy of these gracious and graceful trees for their recovery and well being.

Mother Earth is a sentient being

They are, if you will, a representation of the need for a change in perception of the relationship between your humanity, Mother Nature and Mother Earth for all things must work in harmony, all things must work together for the good of all. Mother Earth must be seen as a sentient being who is treated with respect, love, gratitude and great honour for she is your home, your shelter and your provider.

In the same way that you look after your physical home, clean, polish, tidy, redecorate, repair and so on, to provide a safe and warm home in which to dwell, then so too should you treat Mother Earth with love and respect, care and appreciation, and work in accordance with her needs and desires too.

However, dear friends, all is not doom and gloom, and all is well and all will be well, as we have said before the tide is turning and things are changing and there is now much more light and love flooding your earthly plane in accordance with the Divine Plan, and many more of you are awakening to your true self,to your soul essence of love, and many more are asking what their true path and purpose is within this new energy, this new frequency.

thank the trees

For, dear ones, once you have experienced this new frequency, this new energy, once you have experienced how it feels to be in the new flow of love and light, it is a place where you wish to remain, a place of happiness, love, satisfaction, peace and contentment that you wish to feel on a continual basis. And so, as many of you awaken to your Atlantean energies and your Lemurian energies and reconnect to that true place of love and honouring Mother Earth, of all working together in harmony and respect, then you will automatically move forwards into this new energy.

As your cellular structure releases all that has been held from past accumulated energies, then your body will become lighter and your heart will expand with love and light, and you will experience the glory of the Divine, the glory of the love of God, the glory of All That Is.

And so, dear ones, look forward, look ahead to this wonderful new era that can be yours on this earthly plane.

Thank the trees for the wonderful part they play in the glorious Divine Plan, thank them for their beauty, their grace and their sacrifice, send them love, healing and blessings of gratitude and honour and respect, and know that all will be well and all is well.

Our greatest love."

Insights on Communication

"In this insight on communication, we would wish to share with you all, dear ones, the many forms of communication which are happening on many levels and in many dimensions, and all these forms are occurring at all times, in order to maintain the balance in all things.

For balance is the mainstay of life on your earthly plane, and indeed throughout the universe and beyond, for if things become out of balance this starts and continues a chain reaction which causes ripples that become stronger and stronger until results occur that are disadvantageous to all forms of life, Mother Earth, and beyond your earthly plane.

For your beautiful planet does not exist in isolation, as you are discovering more about the sea-world, the underwater-world, the space beyond your earthly plane, so this creates a rethinking of some data that was taken as factual, and your concepts and awareness must continuously be reviewed, expanded, revised and adapted, and so any truism now or beforehand, may not necessarily always be considered true in the future as more is revealed for you all and your awareness adapts to this new information.

communication between animals

So back to the subject of communication, there are many forms of communication that you now have an awareness of, spoken and non-verbal communications being two of the most obvious; communication via your technology, the text message, the internet and other forms of communications of this sort that are visible and understood.

The awareness that you now have of communications between animals, how many of these creatures are actually more advanced than you anticipated. The communication between bees for example, how do they know where to go to find their food, how do they exchange this knowledge with other bees, indeed how do they store this knowledge into their systems to be transcribed and shared later? How do they adapt to changing circumstances and communicate within the hive to adapt and share these conditions, and make changes to their habits and actions? This wonderfully complex and structured form of communication is just one of many sophisticated ways of communication between animals.

God's law of balance and harmony

Dolphins have an amazingly varied and unique way of communicating, passing this through waters around the world, and passing on to future generations, knowing where to go, knowing when to go, and knowing how to communicate with humankind. To come together in groups, large and small, to share their own wisdom among groups, to transmit the ancient knowledge and wisdom that they have been charged to transfer to each other, and to humankind in these special times. The ability to locate within the vast oceans, the boats and peoples to transfer this information, to pass on all that they have come here to do, to demonstrate their joy and their love for life, for humanity, and for the future of the world.

For it is not by chance that dolphins appear at the side of boats, that they suddenly appear out of the blueness of the waters to leap and dive and display their acrobatic abilities. It is not by chance that they appear beside humankind at different times, for this is their chosen opportunity to transmit their knowledge and wisdom to you all to be passed on to all humanity; to make you aware of the need to look after the God given gifts of the waters and the water-world, the deep seas and oceans, and all the life forms contained within. It is no coincidence at all, dear ones, that you are now learning about these things before it is too late to repair the damage done to Mother Earth, and the dolphins and other sea creatures are helping to raise your awareness that living in harmony is the most important thing; loving, respecting and treating kindly all living beings even those not seen within the waters of the world.

To keep the balance in all things, dear ones, to love, honour, respect, and to treat all things as part of the whole, as part of the oneness, and so as you are part of that oneness, part of the whole, your own well-being and future depends on the balance of all life being kept in accordance with God's law of love, God's law of balance and harmony in all things.

the energies of joy and happiness

And birds, dear ones, we have seen are messengers of the angelic realms, communicating with us again on many levels, helping us to open our minds and awareness to the messages from the angels, the white feathers given to you as signs of love and awareness, signs to remind you to ask for help, signs to remind you to look up to the heavens, to link to the universal energies, to link to the wonders being given and gifted to you from the heavenly realms.

Birds have that special communication of song, of beautiful sounds and vibrations, emitting the light and love of God for you all, and they have the inner awareness and communication of finding their way around the earthly orbit, and if necessary of adapting and changing this in different conditions, and as they express their love of life, as they fly and soar and dive and sing, so they pass on the energies of love and light and joy and happiness to you all, and share the love and wisdom of God with you all.

the balance of all life

And trees, dear ones, plants, flowers, all communicate with you on different levels, they communicate beauty and colour and variety and joy and happiness. Whether in the wild growing naturally and gracefully, whether cultivated in your gardens to bring joy and life and beauty and harmony with all living beings, whether in the house bringing their joy and amazing variety of style, colour, shape, aromas; they are communicating the love of God who created all these things for you, who wants you to be joyful and happy, and share the beauty of all life.

As these plants send roots into the ground they are sharing their energies with Mother Earth, sharing their love and joy of existence with all other living creatures, all other aspects of life that are part of the whole, part of the balance of all life.

As you see the green shoots of Spring, as the leaves begin to reform and uncurl and open out after the winter months, the joy that this communicates to you, the knowledge that the winter is passing, that Spring is on its way once more, that life starts to begin and unfurl and open again, and you can look forward to glorious colours and shapes and trees abundantly full of leaves, glimmering in the sun and fluttering in the breeze. This communication of a new start, a fresh beginning of new possibilities, hope, opportunities, openings, is transmitted to you all, through your eyes, your ears, your sense of smell and touch, through all your beingness to awaken you to a new beginning.

the life cycle of nature

These gracious trees who work to bring new life into the atmosphere, to clear and cleanse the atmosphere for you to breathe in clear healthy air, these gracious, beautiful beings, transmit and communicate the love of God who created them as part of the whole, as part of the structure for allowing and enabling life to exist on this planet, for Mother Earth, who agreed to host the life of these amazing beings and to provide sustenance for them as part of the bigger picture of life on Earth, the picture that encompasses the life of the bees to pollinate, the birds to spread the seeds, to be part of the life cycle of nature to allow and enable life on Earth, to allow and enable you to experience life in a physical form in this existence at this special time in the Earth's history, how magnificent is that?

So, dear ones open your hearts and minds to the various forms of communication that are being made available to you.

These are only a few of the communication systems that exist and are occurring at all levels at this time, we have not in this insight mentioned the crystal world, or other sea-world communications, or the higher levels of communication that occur between you as individuals, but more of that later.

For now, dear ones, we invite you to tune in, open, welcome, all these forms of communication made available to you. Allow in the ancient wisdom and knowledge, the love and light of God that is there for you at all times through all manner of ways, and know that you are so truly loved in all ways, and on all levels; and so until time again, we leave you with our greatest love, dear ones, our greatest love. Thank you."

Insights on Crop Circles

Crop circles have always fascinated me and I love looking at pictures of them. During discussions on these interesting creations at our mediation group Murray suggested I ask The Crystal Team if it would be appropriate to receive some more information.

Here is their insightful reply.

"We are happy to provide some information on Crop Circles and again are pleased to thank our dear Murray for his questions. We are pleased that the UFO information confirmed his own conscious beliefs; and are pleased to answer further questions where the information made available will be appropriate to the current awareness of your conscious/unconscious awareness balance.

Crop circles are shapes, patterns, codes, forms that are indeed a communication system, and are created to bring awareness to you all that there are many aspects of which you do not totally understand, and are not necessarily meant to understand at the time.

they are here for a purpose

Naturally some of these forms are copied or created by your humans and this is not in itself a bad thing as it continues to bring awareness, discussions, media coverage or what you will, about these forms and patterns, and so in this case as you say, no publicity is bad publicity.

However, it does to a small extent, detract from the nature and purpose of these crop circles created especially for the purpose of communication. And by this we mean that not all things are created for reasons that are yet in your conscious awareness but are reminders, or pointers to your subconscious, to those things you know inherently but do not yet know consciously. For on Earth, you cannot yet be in a full state of awareness for this is not the purpose at this time, although many of you are progressing well on the journey to enlightenment and being at one with your true path and purpose.

But the very nature that you are on Earth in a physical form means that you are in a different state with a different purpose that you have chosen to experience here and now in this dimension. So in effect you cannot be in two states at the same time.

And so crop circles, like the feeling you had on UFO's that you believe already, that you know what they are and what they do and why they exist, so too, with crop circles you know subconsciously but this awareness is not yet fully in your conscious mind and so we are unable to pass on too much information at this time.

enjoy their energies

Rest assured that they are here for a purpose, that they are part of the Plan, that more information will be revealed and that you can enjoy the energy of them.

Meditate with their energies, absorb the designs and intricacies of them, enjoy the connection you may feel to them, desire to be more consciously aware of their purpose and meaning but in a light-hearted way. Visit them by all means, and be aware of their energies and allow those energies to make a connection within your systems which will occur naturally and on an unconscious level.

See those shapes, patterns and codes as part of the whole, part of the grid system that exists within the bigger picture. See them as a base or centre, if you will, for communication and know that all is well and all will be well.

With our greatest love."

Colours of Light
A Rainbow Crystal Communication

This Rainbow Crystal resembles a pyramid and looking down
you can see chambers and from the side a palm tree. As I
linked with its energies, I could see the pyramids being built
and feel the heat of the sun and the sand beneath my feet.

Cold as ice, hot as fire, the heat within radiating out and
around
across the Earth and the universe and beyond even that.
The love of God radiating out through the breeze,
through the raindrops, through the rays of the sun.
Feel the rays of the sun warm on your back,
see the love of God in each raindrop and each grain of sand,
feel the love of all that is being gifted to us.

See the pyramid being constructed by advanced science
and thought of mind and intention and desire.
See the love of God in each stage of its development
drafted from seed thoughts and grown with love.
Feel the heat of the sand beneath your feet
and the heat of the midday sun
feel the love of God through all the magnificence of the sun's
rays
helping to construct this creation of devotion and love.

Understand the depth of the inner knowing within the
subconscious
allowing these to be created in fullness
know that this knowledge is still there for you all
know that you can access this intention and information

that as your minds become one with All That Is,
that as you clear all that stands in the way of your total
knowingess that you can access these deepest and innermost
information and intention thoughts
to create your own world of joy and magic.

A oneness that runs across all levels, dimensions, times
to access the knowledge stored within our cells over the
centuries of your time,
for release at the appropriate time for you all.
And that time is emerging, as your crystalline cells open and
blend with our crystalline structures, as your oneness opens
and blends with the oneness that we are all part of,
then you shall access the information, intention and
information that is part of the oneness for all, dear ones, a
oneness that has integrity, love, honesty, openness, truth, trust
and most of all love, at its very centre.

And this can be yours as you open and blend into a state of
oneness
for all times, across all levels and all dimensions.
Your rainbow lights blend with our colours of light,
your cells blend with our cells into the unity of the light,
the unity consciousness of all, of all knowledge, wisdom,
information, intention and love,
as we merge into oneness with the fount of all knowledge,
information and love itself,
into a state of perfection and magnificence, oneness and unity
union.
Ah blessed be."

Experiencing Heaven on Earth

"We are delighted, as always, to communicate these words and energies which will be of great assistance to all your humanity.

For humanity is one kind of life that is available at this present time, and it is one of many opportunities available to us all as a form of soul growth, for, dear ones, we are all on a journey, we are all part of the Master Plan, the Divine Plan, the whole and bigger picture of all that exists, and in this manner we have all experienced many forms of life both in actuality and in physical form.

And as you have become more aware recently, we do not stop loving you all, we do not say "enough" and move away, we do not despair at minor glitches and problems and 'issues' as you call them, for we are aware of the bigger picture, we are aware of the love that is available to you all, if and when, you choose to avail yourself of it.

For love is endless and eternal and as seen by our dear friend Dr Eben Alexander, (author of the book Proof of Heaven) there is a Heaven, there is another level of existence that is wonderful and beautiful, there is another level of energetic reality that is joyful and harmonious. And so as this level of existence and reality is permanent, the love and the joy and peace and harmony that prevails is the reality in that energy dimension.

a love that never goes away

As described by our dear friend so clearly, despite his earthly scepticism, he was reunited for a temporary stage with this reality so that he could describe those beautiful feelings of love, compassion, understanding, care and wisdom that exist in that reality.

And because that existence continues, because it is the essence of where your soul energy originates, it is in your very soul energy, in the existence that you are now experiencing. Your choice to experience life in a physical form was taken with due care and consideration, consultation and discussion as to the reason and benefit for your soul growth and development. And so in the human form, you have the opportunity to reconnect to that soul essence which is in your cellular structure, your DNA, your crystalline grid, and this enables you to feel Heaven on Earth, this enables you to feel that blissful state of joy and harmony, love and peace that is part of who you truly are, the true essence of your soul as part of the bigger picture of love that is the fount of All That Is, that links us all together in the most beautiful way.

your soul energy will grow and glow

This love is so strong and so inherent in your very core existence that it never goes away, it may fade or lose some of its sparkle and shine but it never goes away, and so in your earthly existence, no matter what happens or how bad things appear to be, your strength of love that binds you all together, that binds all levels of existence, that binds all dimensions of existence, is there.

The heartbeat of each and every living being is connected by this love, and as your hearts beat and keep your physical body alive, then so too the love is being continuously circulated around your body and around each and every living being, and this flow of love energy links you and as you breathe it in and take it into your core essence, you are absorbing more of this love energy and circulating more around within the world in which you live for the benefit of all.

And so as you can sense and feel this love is limitless, boundless and inexhaustible because it is the very essence of life itself. And as more of you awaken to your inherent true sense, your core essence, your soul energy, so too will you reconnect to this great store of love that is available, and as your love quotient grows, as your understanding and appreciation grows, then you will feel the love, joy, harmony and peace in all its glory.

Your light will shine brighter, your soul energy will grow and glow, and you will be fulfilling part of your purpose in this earthly existence, and you will feel fulfilled in completing this part of your journey on this earthly plane, and will return to the blissful state of love that is possible to experience here on Earth as well as in Heaven.

And so we thank you all once again, dear ones, for your willingness to be open hearted and to make that reconnection to your core essence of love. We are here to assist you at all times.

With our greatest love."

Insights from the Sea-World

Seahorses - ah blessed be these beautiful creatures of the sea are so graceful and noble. These creatures of light carry the history and wisdom of ancient times and are now becoming more familiar to you as the energies raise in line with the dawn of the new era.

They work in conjunction with dolphins and whales to transmit love and light to all humanity on many levels, through many dimensions.

Their crystalline structure links to the crystal at the heart of the planet and receives messages and energies which are communicated on all these levels for the benefit of all. This radiating of love and light throughout the waters makes connections and communications with sea creatures, plants, water and landmass.

The sea-world is a moving and changing world of great wonder and some mystery yet to be discovered, it holds the remains of ancient civilizations, the knowledge and wisdom and mysteries of these ancient times.

It holds life forms that are as yet unknown to you but which are a vital part of the structure of your physical world and an anchor to all life forms and all beings within.

the wonder of the universe

The beautiful colours, the amazing wonder of the seahorse attracts us to them on a primordial instinct, and we feel drawn to their energies of innocence and wonder. Their movements are also a source of wonder and amazement, and so we are drawn to watch and study and glory in their being which enables a communication to develop at a deep level.

As has been indicated before, much communication occurs on levels that we do not see, hear or are not aware of, so do not question, dear ones, if you are drawn to look at, wonder, admire or study these amazing creatures. Just allow the communication to flow while you take in their magnificence, this magnificence being another gift from God, another aspect of this wonderful life on Earth, another aspect of the wonder of the universe of which, dear ones, you are part of it as it is part of you, and thus you are part of the whole as seahorses are part of the whole.

Enjoy communications and understand that your connection, awareness and understanding of the water-world, and its role as part of the whole, will be growing and developing in a beautiful way."

The Beauty of Life

"We have discussed dear ones, the beauty of life in the time which you call Lemuria, and how the intention and purpose was to lead a 'harmless' life, one which fulfilled the desire to experience life in a physical form, on the earthly plane, whilst not actively creating any undue or harmful influence on Mother Earth while she continued on her own journey and soul growth.

And this required consent and agreement between both these energy essences for this to be continued, and created, for Mother Earth agreed to provide shelter, sustenance, and all other aspects required by the Lemurians for them to have this experience on the earthly plane.

The Lemurians chose to live lightly and harmlessly, fulfilling their desire for this experience, and also gave back to Mother Earth healing of a deep and loving nature, and so the balance of giving and receiving was beautifully maintained and both elements gained greatly from this experience.

In the Golden Age of Atlantis this energy exchange was on a different and more sophisticated level. Mother Earth provided the home, shelter, sustenance and a glorious place in which to exist; she also provided the crystals (different from the Lemurian crystals) which formed a hugely significant part of life in Atlantis, and a different form of balance was achieved between the two energy essences.

sophisticated technology

The Atlanteans used the gifts that Mother Earth provided; they grew crops, used water and other natural materials for buildings, craft and other necessities for their chosen way of life on Earth.

They used crystals for very sophisticated technology which enabled them to have power, heating, lighting and refrigeration. They used crystal technology for transportation, telekinesis and much, much more, yet to be revealed to you, so their lifestyle was very advanced.

However, in accordance with the laws of balance, they took into consideration the ramifications of all their actions, they were aware that each action has a resulting consequence and they desired to keep all actions within the laws of balance and harmony so that all resulting consequences were harmless.

Crystals were used for healing, in agriculture, in childhood development and so on, and were revered, respected, honoured and used with gratitude and appreciation.

life flowed easily

Crystals in agriculture were used in accordance with the seasons, the flow and ebb of the moon energies, with the needs of Mother Earth, and all aspects were taken into account and consideration for the best outcome of all, for maintaining the balance and harmony in all things and for all living beings, and so these intentions and purposes were well-intentioned and pure, and the energies associated with them were pure and beneficial.

Children were taught to respect crystal power and to use them wisely; they understood that these gifts of God were here to help them and appreciated and gave thanks for these powerful beings Mother Earth had graciously allowed for the formation of these crystal gifts, and it was understood that these were being made available as part of the bigger plan, the bigger picture, and were an integral part of their experience.

All decisions on crops grown, on daily living, took into account the needs of the people, the land, the plants, living beings and Mother Earth, and in this way the energies remained high and life flowed easily and joyfully as the balance in all things was maintained.

Balance in giving and taking, balance in appreciation and gratitude, balance in tune with the seasons, balance in tune with Mother Nature, harmony of energies with all people and all living beings, and balance and harmony within the love of God, within the beauty of nature and within our own hearts. A glorious state of beingness!"

Blessings of Love

"Light and love, dear ones, can come in many forms, a gentle touch on your shoulder, a kind word, a smile, a thoughtful deed, the beauty of a flower, the colours of a rainbow; these and many more are all signs of God's love for you all, and we are here for you at all times, all day everyday to tune into and feel the love that exists for you all, with our greatest love and blessings."

This Thing called Love

The Crystal Team comment -

"We do not stop loving you all", "love is endless and eternal", "this love is so strong and so inherent in your very core existence that it never goes away".

But how do we define LOVE, how does it make us feel, and what is it? I wondered if The Crystal Team would like to offer further information and here is their insightful reply.

"We have explained, dear ones, that love is the very heartbeat of life, the very core, the very essence of life on all dimensions, levels and forms of existence.

Love is an energy that is of a very high frequency, that is soft and gentle and yet purposeful and dynamic. It is an energy that flows at a certain level to raise the vibrations of all those who choose to aspire to this level of existence.

This is a choice that you can all make, dear ones, for each day, each moment, each week, each month of your timescale on Earth, you make decisions. What shall I wear, what shall I do, what shall I eat and so too can you choose what do I feel?

All situations and life experience of all levels on your earthly plane can look bad and difficult if looked at in certain ways, and there are many events which do create emotional energies that are genuinely difficult to accept and to deal with.

Once we have an understanding of the bigger picture and the Divine Plan, we can begin to trust in this process that some things happen for a reason, some things turn out for the best, some things can be looked at in many ways. We are not suggesting that all events can be brushed under the carpet, ignored or left un-dealt with, for this is not the intention and may create many difficulties.

allow love to enter any situation

However, if we hold problems, emotions, difficulties up to the light, if we call in assistance, if we pray and if we believe that the intention in the end is to be positive and that a good end result will ensue, then we are holding the space and energy for love to enter the situation.

Lighting candles, prayers, positive thoughts, meditation and contemplation will allow for this positive energy to assist. Pass up the problem, issue, whatever it may be, to the light, see it as part of the bigger picture, allow that we do not have all the answers and allow for love energies to solve and dissolve the negative energy, and allow love to bring peace, compassion, understanding and harmony to all.

Adding negative energies to an issue will increase its volume, will increase the importance of that issue, which make it harder to dissolve and resolve and more problematic for the energy of love to disperse and resolve.

always seek the option of love

The easier it is for the energy of love to flow into the energy of the situation, the sooner it can be resolved. For as you know, we are all energy, we are all one, we are all part of the same, and so adding negative energy to any energy situation creates a lowering of energies for all, whereas adding lighter energies, positivity, hope, compassion, understanding, allows energies to raise to a level where optimism and hope, love and charitability can flow easily and openly, freely and beautifully, clearing away the lower, denser energies lighting the mood, the feel, the intensity of the situation and bringing forgiveness, clarity and peace to you all.

And as more of the love energies are absorbed, understood, shared and accepted so less of the problems arise, less of the difficulties arise, less of the conflicts arise because the low energies cannot exist in the lighter frequency of love.

And this does not mean, dear ones that we can ignore wrong doings, or behaviour that is not acceptable under spiritual law but it gives one the concept on how situations can be resolved when we allow the energy of love to enter and resolve the issue, conflict, problem or whatever else it may be.

So, dear ones, you are invited to always seek the option of love, to always pray for love, to always offer up your problems to love and allow the energies of love to enter, flow, circulate and delight you all and all living beings and Mother Earth."

The Light of God
A Rainbow Crystal Communication

"Pharaoh's and kings, jewels and gems,
gifts from God on high,
shining in the midday sun,
the rays of golden light
warming up the land around and
sending out the signs of light and love
from God above, across all times and lives.

The rainbow lights of love and light
glowing all around
sending beams of light and love
for many miles around
centuries old and history held
within the chamber's walls
communication points around the world

and with the skies above.

Energies from Earth to sky
to the universe and beyond
wisdom, knowledge, future, past,
all linking to the skies
connecting to the energy link
around the galaxies
tuning in, sending out, receiving all the news
of what takes place around our world
and worlds apart in sky.

Knowing, sharing, understanding what and why
things occur on Earth and in the sky,
as all are part of God's creation for us all on Earth
to experience this part of life on our journey's work,
to live and die, to eat and drink,
to breathe and procreate,
as part of our awakening to another level of consciousness
that awaits for us on high.
Moving through times,
moving through the light,
seeing, expanding, growing and awakening
more into the light energies
of what awaits us there,
the love of God, the light of God,
the spark of energy that is part of us and we are part of it.

So see the sun's rays as part of this light,
see the rainbow lights as part of God,
see the pyramids as gifts of knowledge

and wisdom as a gift from God
connecting us to his light and love
and wisdom and knowledge.

See all things connected
and as part of the oneness
and the totality of All That Is.

We are all part of the magic of the light, the oneness,
see yourself in the reflection of the crystal clear waters,
see yourself in the reflection of the rainbow lights
as part of the beauty and oneness of all
for that is who you are dear ones,
that is who you are indeed."

Crystals hold the Secrets of all Life

"We hear you say, dear ones oh this crystal took 3 million years to come into creation, 3 million years or more to form into the beautiful gift that it is.

So as you hold it, feel it, look at it, think and focus on those 3 million years; and this is a long time in your dimension, dear ones.

And think of the changes occurring in your Mother Earth that allowed for this creation, the changes in temperature, in rainfall, in moving continents, in ice ages, in lost ancient civilizations, in underwater worlds, in mountain creations and movements, in life forms, in colours and shapes, and in connections to the outer reaches of life on other planets and other galaxies.

crystals create magic

Think of these things, dear ones, as you hold and look at this perfection within your hands, and wonder at the gifts it brings you. Wonder at the colours, the energies, the forms, the love of God, the love of Mother Earth, the love of the universe and beyond.

And think of all that occurred to allow this creation to occur, and your crystal being will link your energies to Mother Earth in a magical way that will bring you strength, love, understanding, awareness and joy.

For how can you not have greater understanding and awareness when you hold this crystal that holds the secrets of Mother Earth; her history, her joy, her life plan, her awareness of being part of the bigger picture?

How can your understanding and appreciation not increase exponentially when you link to these energies, histories, and love?

How can you not strengthen your connection to Source who envisioned the creation of these beings ready for this time on Earth for you to access and benefit from at this special time on Earth?

How can you not marvel at how all this fits together as part of the magic of the Divine Plan for you all?

talk to them

These crystals hold the secrets of the future and the past, they hold the ancient wisdom and knowledge of what has been and what can be, they are the record keepers, the knowledge keepers, and they are your guides and teachers, they are your friends and your advisers, they can help you reach awareness and understanding on unimaginable levels to you at present.

They are the past, present and future wisdoms of all beings, on all times, levels, dimensions; they are Mother Earth's gifts to you, dear ones.

Work with them, love them, talk to them, listen to them and appreciate and be grateful for these amazing beings. Thank them for their agreement to act as transformers of knowledge and wisdom, as timekeepers and record holders, and work with them with an open mind and an open heart. And we watch with great excitement as your intuition expands, your inner knowingness grows and your heart develops to its fullest potential on all levels, across all times and dimensions, now and forever more amen."

Simple Prayers

"We unite in prayers dear ones so that the combined energy and intention are magnified by the love and dedication of all souls involved.

And this may not need to be a long session of prayer; a minute or two are enough to add to the energy intention of your focus.

So prayers for yourself, your loved ones, Mother Earth, for abundance in all things, for world peace and so on, could be as simple as:-

I pray for peace within my heart and within the heart of all
living beings,
Mother Earth and beyond.
May the loving abundance of the universe deliver all that is
desired
within God's Law of rightfulness.
Amen.

Be light-hearted in your prayers and know that they are heard. Be patient and remain loving to yourself and all others.

With our greatest love to you all. Amen."

Connecting to the Energies of Love
A Beautiful Meditation from The Crystal Team

This beautiful meditation has been communicated to allow us to feel, sense, absorb and integrate the energies of love, to bring into every cell of our body, the greatest gift of all, the love of God.

And this can be experienced either sitting outside in the warmth so you can be at one with nature, or sitting inside with some gentle music, and perhaps a candle. Choose a time when you will not be disturbed, choose your favourite crystals to work with, and when you are comfortable imagine strong white roots growing from the souls of your feet going deep down into Mother Earth, knowing that she will hold you in her loving energies. Ask the angels to be with you while you enjoy this meditation, and surround the room you are in with golden, shimmering, shining light which allows in only the energies of the highest Divine order.

"Enjoy this meditation and know that we are with you at all times."

★★★★★★★★★★

"We would invite you, dear ones, to rest yourselves upon the ground, to sit on a rug or a warm patch of grass, to make yourself at ease and comfortable, to allow yourself the time to take time out from your daily life, and to have the intention of connecting to the Divine, connecting to the essence of All That Is, the essence of love that is available to you all.

As you sit upon the grass or chair, allow yourself to relax, to switch off from all those aspects of your daily life that you can put aside for a few moments. They will still be there for you to collect later, although they may not have the same importance or relevance when you revisit them.

So allow your mind to leave the daily affairs aside, allow your breath to become deep and slow and even, allow the very breath of life, the very breath of God, your provider, to fill every cell in your body, to fill all your senses, to fill every space in your aura.

Feel that love filling every part of you as you breathe it in. Sense, feel and know that this God, Source, Manna and provider loves you all so much, loves you so much as to provide you with this experience on Earth that you have chosen at this special time, to be a part of the changing times and energies here on Earth.

How does this love feel to you? Is it soft and warm like a gentle breeze?

Does it have an aroma like a delicate rose scent?

Does it have a colour; perhaps a beautiful shade of pink or blue or purple?

Does it shine and shimmer?

Does it have a sound like fairy laughter or a gentle stream?

Does it make you feel soft and relaxed or happy and joyful?

Really get a sense of how this love feels to you.

And as you really connect with these energies of love, the energy essence of God, the God of love, the God who is love, then see this love energy being taken into your body, into every cell in your lungs and into your blood stream; see it flowing round your body, clearing and cleansing, revitalising, rejuvenating, healing, energising as it flows round.

See your body responding to this love, see it relaxing, and letting go of all that no longer serves you, who you are today or who you wish to be.

See it activating the ancient wisdom and knowledge within your cells, your cellular structure, and your crystalline grid.

See the tension dissolving from your muscles, and the toxins being transported away for clearance, see your body glowing and shinning, radiant, healthy, clear, pure and beautiful.

See your eyes shining clearly so they can see the truth and the light.

See your ears clear, so they can hear the truth, and see your throat clear and open so you can speak the truth and your truth.

See your body well, healthy and happy so you can join in and be part of all that you wish to do as part of your personal journey. See your heart lift and gladden at the purity of the love flowing through it.

See your lungs breathing easily and deeply, absorbing all the clear pure air and love, and exhaling all the energies that can be safely released for transmutation.

See your hands flexible and ready to do those tasks that are part of your own journey, uniting you to your own true soul essence.

See your feet strong and steady, supporting you in all you have chosen to do at this exciting time on Earth, and allowing you to freely move forwards into the new era, the new times ahead.

And see all your body aglow with the love and light of God, for as your light shines brighter, so too you will inspire and ignite in others the desire to move forwards into the new energies, to assist them to reunite with their memories of the golden days of Atlantis and Lemuria where life was joyful and harmonious.

And as you continue to take in the love and light of God, the beauty of all that surrounds you and all that is being made available to you, then you are strengthening your connection to God, Source, Manna, the Great Provider in the most glorious way, and your life will flow more easily and harmoniously and joyfully.

Enjoy being in these beautiful energies, dear ones, before returning to your everyday life and resuming your normal beingness, and know that you have received the greatest gift of all in great abundance, and may your day be filled with joy and happiness, love and laughter. We wish you well, dear ones, with our greatest love."

The Grace of God

A Rainbow Crystal Communication

"I am the living embodiment of clarity and light formed over many millennia,
through movements and changes in the Earth's beingness,
formed for love and with love,
formed from the Grace of God for you all.
Heat and cold, dry and wet, wind and storm, sand and grain shaped and shifted into perfection,
into love personified in an ancient form for humanity at the new dawn of time.

Embodied with light, with love, with clarity, honesty,
openness and information for you all,
connect into my inner wisdom, absorb my energies,
integrate them into your cellular structure and your crystalline
beingness.
Make those connections of energies, memories, of times past
and times ahead,
absorb the intention and the information,
and the passion, and the glory that God has created for you.
Release through your beingness all that no longer serves you,
all that holds you back from being who you truly are,
and allow your glorious beingness to shine with clarity,
brightness and joy.

Be at one with all the elements of all living beings, of all
beingness in this universe,
and the universes beyond your understanding.
Feel yourself as part of the oneness,
the wholeness, the unity of All That Is,
marvel in the wonders of the world around you,
breathe them in and express your gratitude for all that is being
made available to you all
for there is much joy, dear ones, much joy for you all.

And we bless you and encourage you to accept and experience
this joy
as part of your experience in this lifetime that you have chosen
at this exponentially exciting time on Earth.
We bless you, we love you, and we are part of you,

we are part of the oneness, the greatness, the wonder of All that Is,
and working in harmony with all aspects of life, seen, unseen, understood and not understood.
When you hurt another energy being you are in effect hurting your own being,
and so be aware of your oneness, your unity, your grace, and All Will be Well, and All Is Well.

We bless you, we salute you, and we are with you always, till time again. Amen."

The Body's Ability to Heal itself through Self-communication

"We have indicated that you have all you need to help to restore and rebalance your energy field, for remember that you are primarily energy, and God in his love for humanity has given and prepared for the restoration of rebalance to all manifestations of energy.

And especially at this time on Earth which is both exciting and demanding of your focus and energies to carry forward the commitment that you all agreed to do in this lifetime and against opposition and negativity and suspicion and scorn, you are all working to shine your light in a most glorious way for the benefit of all.

As your light shines, so you assist others on an unconscious level, to change also in their energy field to begin to wake up and to reconnect with their own remembrances and agreements with All That Is.

threads of energy

Energy works on many levels, there are personal energies which can easily become unbalanced and dis-energised by environment, pollution, people's energy, the weather, the moon and many other aspects.

There are the universal energies that are governed by the planets in your system, by the outer galaxies and by Mother Earth and out into the beyondness, and these are affected by the crystal resonance of all that is occurring at all times and levels of beingness and timelessness.

Within this there is a constant thread of energy, a constant link with the founder of All That Is, with the provider of all your experiences, the provider of Mother Earth for you to have this experience, for the provider of all that you have experienced, and all that you are experiencing, and all that you may experience in other dimensions.

manifestations of nature

And so this link is constant, nothing can alter this thread, this link, this energy system that links all humanity together through every cell of your being through every part of your body, your crystalline grid and your genetic make-up.

Each person as an individual manifestation of energy, as a soul being experiencing life on Earth at this time, is also an exact replica of the energy make up of the energy of God – how could it be otherwise when you are all created by the same magnificent source for the same purpose at this time in your timeframe?

And so to strengthen your connection to this source is to strengthen your connection to the source of your very beingness, the source of your origin, conception, physicality and soul level of existence. It is like plugging into the mains power, through using all the gifts at your disposal, all the gifts that are made available to you; crystals, nature of all aspects, communications within the natural world to assist your understanding and connection, these manifestations of nature as part of yourself, of connecting if you like, to other members of your family, to other parts of yourself.

So you can gain strength on a physical level and also on an emotional level, feeling part of something bigger, a bigger family if you like, so each flower, tree, bird, animal, blade of grass and so on is another part of you, another link that unites you in oneness, another part of your family – the family of God.

be embraced by the wings of love

So would you hurt or mistreat another part of your family, or would you prefer to spend time with it, exchanging nice thoughts, appreciation for its beauty and purpose? Would you nurture it and feed it and look after it, would you admire it and welcome it as part of yourself, would you connect to it to bring love, support, joy into your world like other family members would?

You have access to parts of nature at all times via photo's, videos, pictures, real physical beings, listening to bird song, reading about them, see how easy it is to link, connect, join, in energies and physical contact with these elements of nature?

Your souls have become so disjointed and unconnected from their true origin, from their family members, from the strength of their energy source, and have sought comfort, solace and energy from unreliable sources; and these sources are now becoming exhausted and complicated and in turmoil, but dear ones, you have the answer at your fingers tips, through your eyes, your senses, your thoughts, your intentions, your communications, through beauty, through colour, through the sounds of the trees rustling in the breeze, the warmth of the sun, the light of the night sky. You have it all dear ones, and it is free, accessible and amazingly beautiful.

Making these connections, uniting with your extended family in other energy forms, uniting with all aspects of your creator and linking to your original energy source will bring you back into balance, at one with seasonal variations, renewal, regeneration.

Refreshed, your soul will be at peace and filled with the love of God, the warmth of the love that is available to you, you will not need to seek unreliable and unsustainable energy sources outside of your soul level, and will be strong, wholesome, united and unified in this love, support, cherishment and embraced by the wings of love, and the care and inspiration available to you.

And so sit quietly, surrounded by lovely music, aspects of nature, and invoke the love of God to assist you to make that connection to Source.

INVOCATION

I now renounce all other forms of energy than that which I know to be true.

I now accept the love of God as my provider of all my experiences.

I now invite the love of God to fill every part of my being, and make the connection to every cell of my being as created by God.

I now invite and welcome the loving energy of God to link and unite all these aspects of my soul that are in truth, honesty, openness, sanctity and oneness.

I now unite in the love of God all aspects of my being as created from the start of time to bring my being into true alignment with God's love so that I may be whole, complete, loving, joyful, and be in balance with my energy field at all times, living in a state of grace, love, peace, compassion, helpfulness, sincerity, and bliss. I now ask for this to be complete in the name of God. Amen."

The Way Forward To Peace on Earth Is Now Set

"At this exciting time on Earth, there are many aspects to celebrate and see as confirmation that the Divine Plan exists for all humanity, Mother Earth and beyond. This Plan was created before humankind, before the creation of the Earth, and was created as a blueprint for soul growth and soul expansion.

Events have unfolded over many timeframes, and we are now at a point where the energies are increasing in line with the expansion of the crystalline grid which holds the light and love of God for us all. In 2012 two significant events occurred and this was possible due to the dedication and commitment of many souls who worked to bring in, hold and expand the light quotient to sufficient levels to allow for these events. On 12.12.12 the 144 crystalline grid was established allowing the structure for the light to flood into the Earth orbit on 21.12.12; and this magnificent event holds the blueprint allowing peace on Earth to become possible.

The way forward to peace on Earth is now set, and is possible within the heart and mind of all souls on Earth, and events are continuing to unfold which allow for all souls to release all that no longer serves them in these changing times, it allows for the release of all which prevents us from following our true path and purpose in this lifetime, and which prevents us from experiencing our true soul essence, our true soul energy.

we are crystalline beings

For as all souls are linked within the light and love of God as part of the oneness of All That Is, then all souls are sparks of light and love held within the heart and mind of God, and allowing your true soul essence to shine through creates a life on Earth of true magnificence, a life of love, harmony, clarity, equality, joy, abundance for all, and this allows for peace on Earth, now and forever more.

Establishing the crystalline grid to a level of such magnitude forms the framework for the Plan to unfold. As we are crystalline beings, as our planet is crystalline, then again we are all inextricably linked on many levels, and as we clear our ancestral and current miscreations, so we allow our crystalline essence to shine brighter and become more pure in essence.

As we link to the crystals within the Earth, as we work with the crystals in a physical form, given to us as a gift from God, so we become beacons of the light and love of God who created this realm for us to experience a spiritual existence within a physical form, an opportunity for soul growth and expansion within the earthly realm. And so as the Plan unfolds, as we find our way forward into the light and love of God, there will be peace on Earth. Amen."

A Few More Words on Love

"Love, dear friends,
is like a gossamer thread that binds you all together.
It is light, bright, sparkly, shiny, colourful and joyful.
It connects you all on the earthly plane
with lightness and joyousness;
the connections spread far and wide
to all aspects of your spiritual connections,
it spreads far and wide
to all aspects of your emotional connection,
and it spreads far and wide
to all aspects of your mental essences.

And these connections spread far and wide
around your earthly plane,
and far and wide into your solar system,
your galaxies, your constellations and beyond.
The stars twinkle and shine with love,
the sun burns brightly with love,
the moon shimmers and shines with love.

Your God and fount of all love,
radiates powerful love to all aspects of life,
seen and unseen, understood and not understood.
The love may fade
between elements of your humanity,
but the love never disappears,
the love may appear to dim

and the light be less visible,
but rest assured the love is always there.

For how can it not be, dear ones,
when God loves you all
and wants the very best for you all?
And how is the love demonstrated
to you all on Earth?
With the beauty and grace of Mother Earth
to provide you with a shelter,
a home, with sustenance and water,
to allow your existence and purpose
for this lifetime to occur.

And the love that created the crystals
with all their power and glory
to allow for the technology in Golden Atlantis,
this power that can be yours again
if used in the appropriate way
for the betterment of life for you all.
The crystals which are healing all mankind
on a conscious and unconscious level
at this special time for you all.

The crystals that allow for healing
within Mother Earth,
to allow her to move forwards on her journey,
the beauty of the crystals which allow healing
on a personal level for you all.
The love of God which forgives all perceived ills

and makes no judgements,
the love of God that welcomes all living beings,
in all its forms,
the love of God that is the Creator of all things.

And so, dear ones, do not fear that love
will ever run out or disappear or falter,
for this cannot be the case.
Love on a grand scale is available to you all,
open your hearts, breathe in the beauty of life,
breathe in the beauty of all
that has been provided for you,
breathe in the love that abounds in all your soul essence,
your cellular structure, your DNA, your crystalline grid.

Allow that love to permeate
every cell of your body,
and see yourself radiating love
to all around you, to all living beings,
to your beautiful planet
and to Mother Earth and out into the universe.

How beautiful and magnificent a sight is that, dear ones? How magnificent for you all!"

Being in the Bubble of Balance and Harmony

"We have spoken previously about maintaining balance and harmony in all aspects of your life, and in this communication we wish to reveal further information of how this can be achieved, and the benefits to yourself and all around you, as you work towards this intention.

Maintaining balance and harmony is a place of beingness where the energy feels stable, calm, purposeful, clear and light. To be able to see things from a higher perspective, whether you use the image of a high wire act, or place yourself as if on a cloud looking down, you are distancing yourself, if you will, from the possible maelstrom of emotions and chaos that might be occurring around you.

It is very easy and quite natural to become involved in discussions, to make opinions, to give judgements about events and issues, and this is part of your experience of humanity to assess and judge events.

However we would also advise caution about becoming involved in too much discussion, judgement and opinion because it adds energy to the situation which already carries a negative stance.

And so by acknowledging the issue or situation and accepting that it exists, it is then possible to aspire to step back and place yourself at a distance from the strength of the emotions involved, and then to place yourself at an energetic level that feels peaceful and harmonious, and from this point to make a reaction, a considered thoughtful reaction about your course of action and language.

balance and harmony

When we react quickly in the heat of the moment it is easy to say words whose intention is not going to help, it is not going to create an atmosphere of trust and calm, it is more likely to add fuel to the fire and ignite more unpleasant words, thought and actions. And this can then also have long lasting consequences.

When you aspire to place yourself in the energies of balance and harmony you are holding the intention of love, holding the intention of light and brightness, to create a reaction that is thoughtful and of benefit to all concerned. This does not mean that you are unfeeling, or cold, or distant from the emotional turmoil of others or indeed yourself, it just means that you have the intention of resolving the issue in the best possible way for all parties, and thus prevent an escalation of negative energies which can be very harmful.

And we do not suggest that this can be achieved easily, for we have our own internal dialogue to consider, our own emotional responses that are triggered from our own weakness, hurts, disappointments and sadness's, but if we aspire to place ourselves in the bubble of balance and harmony, we have set the intention of being fair, open, honest and non-judgemental, of leaving our own weaknesses aside, and seeing impartially what is the best course of action and the most appropriate words to use. And in this your body language and your energetic presence will alter to one of more peaceful energies, and this will also help the situation, for as we know dear ones, our bodies are wonderful representations of our emotional state and can reveal much about us. When our words and our energy states are in harmony and balance, we are calmer, more considered, more peaceful and our words have more significance and will be received more subtly on many levels.

So, dear ones, are you beginning to see how it is possible, and to see how beneficial it is, to place yourself in a position of balance and harmony? And in this way, harmful words may be left unsaid, situations will repair more easily, you will have protected your energy field from the damage of harmful thoughts and emotional reactions, and you will have helped the other person/people to resolve the issue in a way that demonstrates a peaceful resolution can be a successful resolution for all concerned.

ask for help

And in this way, Mother Earth will not be absorbing more negativity, for once negativity is displayed it cannot be retracted and must needs go somewhere, and more balance and harmony will allow all people, all living beings and Mother Earth to remain also in a state of balance and harmony, to continue on that journey to reconnect to their soul essence, their soul energy as part of the whole, as part of the oneness. So your intention of aspiring to hold the light in all situations is a grand statement within a much bigger scale of events, and one that is appreciated on all levels, and in all dimensions.

Ask for our help, dear ones, you are not expected to do this alone, there is much help available to you, nor are you expected to be perfect, nor achieve this state of balance and harmony in one fell swoop as you say. However aspirations of this kind are very noble aspirations and one which will benefit you greatly, helping you to keep your focus, helping your physical, emotional, mental and spiritual bodies to remain balanced, harmonious, happy and healthy.

Congratulate yourself each time you aspire to remain in a state of balance and harmony, and know that each time you do this it becomes easier until you constantly desire to be in this state, in these beautiful energies, where life flows and opens up before you in the most wonderful way.

And as more people reach this state of lightness, brightness, as more people connect to the light and love of God, then peace will descend on Earth, dear ones, for chaos and turbulence cannot survive in the energies of balance and harmony. Peace on Earth is possible, dear ones.

With our greatest love."

Insights on Animal Communication (Dogs)

"This is a particularly interesting and in-depth communication as dogs have many purposes in this lifetime, and have offered to play a major role in the awareness and development of humanity.

As has been said before, humankind are not the only intelligent life form on Earth, they may think they are but it depends on how you quantify and measure intelligence and how this intelligence supports your life on Earth and supports your spiritual development and understanding.

When intelligence is concerned with measuring memory, reading and understanding and repeating facts and using this to create more materialistic goods, wealth and status, this is not true intelligence because anything that creates an imbalance within the Earth, creates an imbalance within the energetic resonance of the Earth, and is not intelligence because it actually harms all living beings and Mother Earth and beyond.

When intelligence is used to create inequality, injustice, unfairness, divided societies, racism, poverty and conflict how can this be a useful form of intelligence when it is not for the highest and greatest good of all?

When information and data are gathered and used to create dissatisfaction, discontent, hatred, extremes of wealth and extremes of poverty, abandonment and ill-health, how can this be intelligence used in a way that creates a harmonious, joyful society where people work together happily, peacefully, in equality, fairness, peace, honesty and love for each other and Mother Earth?

joy and delight

And so we suggest that animals have an intelligence or inherent sense that enables them to live according to their environment, to adapt, to work according to the laws of nature, and when left to themselves would have that balance of evolution and existence in accordance with the Divine Plan without assistance from mankind.

Animals are killed for survival as part of this Plan but otherwise are allowed to live their life as ordained and rear their young in peace. This innate sense or internal ability allows the peaceful co-existence of many species to experience what they have come here to do. There is no hierarchical sense of greatness, control, unfairness or injustice within this way of life.

Compare this to the existence of mankind where there are imbalances within the energetic resonance of existence on many levels.

So as said before, horses are able to use their inner abilities to assist humans, to bring healing on many levels, to calm and soothe, to open their heart centres, to communicate on unspoken levels which other human beings cannot yet do.

Birds are messengers from above, their communication systems are highly developed, their ability to bring joy and delight as they swoop and dive through the sky, their innate ability to fly long distances to other countries without navigation, their ability to bring many messages which are picked up by certain souls, all these show their intelligence allows them to exist independently within their own remit, and touch the hearts of people around the world.

patience and dedication

Dogs are in particular very special beings who have offered to be of service to humanity in many ways.

Their communication systems are incredible, their senses are finely tuned, and their hearts are huge and lovingly open to all humanity. They have agreed to be domesticated to assist humanity at this exciting time, and their gifts to humanity are generously given.

Dog spirits have agreed to be trained to assist those who cannot see; their patience and lovingness is a great comfort and support to many souls, and they work together on an energetic level of obedience, understanding, generosity and love.

Their ability to be trained for this work is a gift in itself, and not all dog spirits are agreeable to this as it is very demanding work for them, but experienced spirit souls agree to be part of this group of service work and are happy to work with their chosen soul mate in this instance.

 The bond between the dog spirit and the person is of such trust and partnership as is mutually beneficial to both participants. The trainers of these dog spirits also work on very fine energetic levels, and we applaud the patience and dedication of all those involved with this rewarding work.

Dog spirits also agree to be domesticated as pets to bring love, comfort, enjoyment and happiness to many people, individuals and families alike. Their energy is soothing and calming in stressful times and joyful and fun at others, they can sense changes in atmosphere and through this are able to bring comfort and solace in difficult times.

service to humanity

Their ability to know when their owners are due home, their ability to find their way back home, the legendary rescues made by dog spirits, the finding of people stranded in difficulty, alerting people of dangers or others in need of help, all demonstrate their intelligence in using their senses and trusting their instincts.

Dogs can often reflect the personalities of those they live with, and this can be a gift reflecting back to their human something that they may wish to work on, acting like a mirror to them. We are all here to learn, develop and grow, and anything mirrored back to us is an opportunity to look at this aspect of ourselves and decide whether to take action upon it.

Dog spirits have also agreed to work as rescue dogs in many situations, and again they are willing to use their many senses in an intelligent way to assist in rescuing people in difficult situations. They can be trained very highly; however they still need to combine the innate energetic ability with a process of individual intelligence to affect the rescue.

In the same way they are trained to discover unwanted illegal substances, and work in detection in conflict zones; this willingness to be of service to humanity is a great gift indeed. Their willingness to be of service in whatever capacity it is still requires a love for the highest and greatest good of all, an innate intelligence, and sense of responsibility and commitment.

We take this opportunity to deeply express our gratitude to all dog spirits who have agreed to be of service to humanity in whatever form that is, and for their willingness and commitment to work for the highest and greatest good of all. For in serving humanity they are raising the energies of all people, all living beings and Mother Earth, and as part of the overall raising of energies, and as part of the Plan moving into the new era of enlightenment and unity, and this service work is of untold value.

And so dear ones, we see that animals have an intelligence and ability and a deeply loving soul which is an essential part of the whole that you exist within.

intelligent intelligence

It is time in this new era, that this ability, devotion, commitment and intelligence of the animal kingdom is recognised.

Many of you already appreciate the sympathetic, empathetic intelligence of the natural world, and as your understanding increases and your awareness grows, so you will see more and more how you are all linked within life on Earth, and how it is possible to co-exist in a wonderful way which honours all souls, human or animal, which allows for harmony among all aspects of life on Earth, which allows for great co-operation between all worlds, and so benefits all living beings and Mother Earth.

Intelligent intelligence used creatively and wisely with great understanding and awareness for the benefit of all will create a world of joy, harmony, beauty, peace, enjoyment and enlightenment, and this is possible dear ones, as part of the unfolding Plan, it is indeed magnificently possible for you all.

Mankind has a great intelligence, a great ability to learn, discover, understand and utilise this information, and when this is used for the highest and greatest good of all with the understanding of the bigger picture, the common unity of all living beings, the oneness of All That Is, how amazing that will be, and we await the development of all this with great excitement.

Adieu for now dear ones; enjoy your contact and relationship with all animals, and blessed be to you all, open your hearts to the love that is available to you from all forms, and your life will be enhanced beyond measure."

Pyramids – a link between Heaven and Earth

"These ancient artefacts or constructions are a part of the history and structure of your world; they are part of the geometric design, the energy system and the pattern of life on Earth.

Their connections to all aspects of life, and life beyond the earthly plane, are magnificent, and they have withstood the passing of the ages to be here in your present timeframe to help you reconnect to all the ancient wisdom and history that is part of your very beingness.

For all shapes and symbols have energy and meaning. We know that the infinity energy is one of continuity, of shadow and light, of past, present and future, of all things held in balance, in equality, now and forever more.

We know that sounds have shapes and resonance; we know that images can be demonstrated on a physical level to show those patterns and forms.

We know that harmonious sounds resonate with the body's frequency to bring peace, healing, soothing and relaxation, they calm the mind, heart and soul, and so bring joy, peace and happiness.

commonality and balance

We know that water has a frequency, a memory system, and an energy that brings clarity, clearing, cleansing and purity. The sound of water running in a stream, the sound of gentle waves rippling on the beach, even waves crashing in a storm, all bring resonance, clearing and energies to the Earth, and all who live on her.

We know that crystals have their own frequency to bring the body's energy field into balance and harmony. The constant structure within the crystal brings uniformity, commonality and balance; the minerals within the crystal add qualities to assist humanity to heal wounds of emotional and physical sources, to bring in qualities that assist in spiritual awareness and mental calmness.

We know that geometric shapes bring energies of their own, and when drawn or imagined will assist in bringing creativity, balance, harmony and joy.

And so, all aspects of life begin to demonstrate to your growing awareness, that there is a meaning and a purpose in everything; all these gifts are created by God, Source, the Great Provider, to assist in all ways, at all times, to benefit from.

Shapes are repeated throughout nature, throughout buildings, throughout your own physicality, and all support your existence and awareness to continue on your journey and to be in alignment with All That Is and your true path and purpose. It is another aspect of oneness, another aspect of being part of a bigger picture, of a system of intelligence that has created all this on Earth for you at this time.

And so to return to the pyramids, a shape and form that is made up of several shapes and forms, and when constructed together creates a multi-layered pattern that holds and retains the energy; a link between Heaven and Earth, a repository, a holding station, a beacon, and a chamber of healing.

Pyramids can be built in alignment with the stars to track the energy of the moving sky; as all is in alignment with the oneness, then all is connected through all levels and layers of existence.

Atlantean wisdom

Tracking the movements of the sun and stars enabled the Atlantean wisdom carried through to Egypt to construct giant crystal edifices atop the pyramids to absorb and contain the energy to be converted into domestic use, for healing, for use in agriculture, and many other uses. For crystal power generated in this way was pure, controllable, beneficial; with none of the pollutants that are experienced by your modern methods of generation of power.

The communication between these pyramid constructions enabled power to be stored and shared among all areas like you have substations today, and by design of the placing of the pyramids and the caretaking of the crystals, this power was naturally available at all times, and it was accepted with gratitude and appreciation.

And again the construction of the pyramid by adjustment to the design, allowed for a healing chamber to be created. As said before, sound has a frequency and when that frequency resonates with the human energy field, it can help bring it back into balance as a conductor uses a tuning fork to bring the orchestra into balance. And so sound chambers of different frequencies were available to assist all people, and in this chamber colours were used as colour also has a frequency and an energy that supports and encourages emotional and spiritual, mental and physical balance, and so moving colours accompanied the sound and crystals could also be used to amplify both colour and sound in these chambers.

Can you imagine how glorious it would be to be in a sacred space of careful construction, dedicated to the healing of all souls? And within this chamber, harmonious sounds floated around you while beautiful colours moved slowly throughout, and all this enhanced and amplified by the healing, rebalancing energies of crystals. Can you dear ones, get a sense of the beauty and restorative qualities of this experience?

awakening to this knowledge

And so as has been shown that using a pyramid shape can help to maintain the nutritional quality of food when stored within its energy, so the energies can repel or discourage insects to venture inside, so this all demonstrates that this shape has an energy of its own that is unique and wonderful. A pyramid built on a dedicated sacred place, built with love and constructed by ingenuity, intention, thought and crystal technology creates a magnificent energy which could be adapted to its own particular usage.

All these gifts dear ones keep demonstrating to you how benevolent your creator is in gifting these things to you, and in providing Mother Earth who generously agreed to allow humanity to have the experience of life on Earth.

How can all this be random dear ones, how can all this be a lucky chance of circumstances that you have everything you need to be happy, balanced, joyful and live in harmony, all within your own knowledge and awareness?

As more souls awaken to this knowledge and wisdom, as more souls connect to the collective light, so you will move towards the understanding and appreciation of all that is being made available to you, and to the magnificent lifestyle that can be created when the collective light shines as one bright light for all humanity.

Look around you dear ones, see how much connectivity there is in existence, see how all things are cause and effect, linked, joined and united in oneness, now and forever more, Amen.

Our greatest love to you all, and we delight in seeing your continued expansion and joy as your awareness and understanding flourish and grow.

Adieu dear ones, adieu."

A Message of Joy

"As always it is our joy and our privilege to share these words and energies with you all for joy is what it is all about.

Joy of experiencing a physical life on Earth.

Joy of nature and all the beauty of the gifts of nature; the trees, the bird song, the waters in all their forms flowing gracefully and glinting in the sunshine.

Joy of the shapes and forms that make the foundations of your life on Earth, the corner stones, if you will, upon which all things are created, and all things mirrored and reflected throughout all life forms, all living beings, Mother Nature and the Earth itself.

Joy of a cloudless sky, a sunset and sunrise.

Joy of the shadows as the sun moves across the clouds.

Joy of the moon beaming her golden light and bringing in her divine feminine energies and ancient wisdoms.

Joy of being with your family and friends, recognising your soul counterparts and seeing the love of God through the eyes of all souls reflected back to you.

Joy of the love of God who created all this for you.

Joy of the life of Jesus Christ who came to Earth to show you the way forward.

Joy of a cool breeze on a hot day.

Joy of the sound of rain to water the grass and fill the reservoirs.

Joy of the energies of crystals and crystal skulls to assist you on your journey and bring beauty to your life.

Joy of sitting in quiet contemplation and allowing your mind to still.

Joy of being at peace with yourself and others.

Celebrate these reasons to be joyful and know that we are with you, celebrating and enjoying your delight in these gifts.

And in this way you will be raising the energies of all living beings, of all life forms and Mother Earth to assist in bringing joy and inner peace and stillness to all others as we move towards the prophesied time of peace on Earth.

Celebrating this joy will bring you closer to Source/God who created all this for you, as you open your heart centres to these gifts, to the energies of these gifts, so your heart centre resonates with the energies of love and light at the heart centre of your creator, your provider of all your experiences, in this and all your lifetimes, world without end, Amen.

Enjoy and celebrate, strengthen your connection to the oneness of All That Is for the benefit of yourself and all others; there is nothing selfish in doing this, you are going beyond your-self to connect to the heart centre of the creator of All That Is, and that dear ones is the greatest gift of all.

And so with our greatest love as always, be joyful, until time again. Amen.

A State of Grace

"Our message today, dear ones, is about balance and harmony with all things. This essence has been described in other insights in many different forms, and this insight will demonstrate more on the importance of maintaining balance and harmony within yourself and this then enables and empowers souls to actively pursue balance and harmony in all things.

For, dear ones, if you can imagine a high wire act, a person balancing on this precarious perch high above a ravine or other place of perceived danger, then it is important for that person to remain balanced and focussed at all times. One slip or loss of focus and balance would have disastrous effects if not rectified swiftly.

And it is also essential to be in harmony with all things, for being in harmony with the elements of wind, sun, temperature, harmonious with himself, for any disturbance in his energy field would create lack of focus leading to possible consequences.

Now, dear ones, your life is not quite such a high stress balancing act but it is a balancing act of sorts throughout all your life, and the decisions you make, the thoughts you have, and the deeds you undertake all are part of that balancing act of harmony, of energies to keep you focussed on your reason for being on this earthly plane, at this special time on Earth.

universal energies of space

And Mother Earth also has a balancing act to consider. She has agreed and consented to allowing life on Earth, to allowing for humanity to have this experience at this time, to provide shelter, sustenance and love for all humanity, all living beings, and maintain her connections within the universe for keeping the balance in the bigger picture.

She also has her own agenda if you like, her own path to ascension, her own soul journey to follow, and this is important for her development, and therefore much focus and consideration must be given to this. And all forms of life seen and unseen, understood and not understood, are also to be considered and balanced, for these also have an effect on her energies.

And so can you see, dear ones, that as part of the universe, as part of the greater aspect which you call space, Mother Earth has an important part to play; one which she takes seriously as part of her contract for times ahead. So it is not just humanity that has needs and considerations to balance; and all plants, animals, and beings of light also play a part, and have needs and life paths to follow and consider as part of Mother Earth's journey to ascension.

So humanity would do well to consider the implications of all their thoughts, deeds, plans and intentions, for the resulting outcomes will not only affect them, but all living beings, Mother Earth and the universal energies of space.

So can you now see that the balancing act of the high wire exercise is very similar to that of the balancing act of life, for if all things are not taken into consideration then the focus is lost, the balance is unstable, and if left uncorrected can have disastrous results.

the love and light of God

Now we do not wish to frighten, scare or be negative in any way. The light and love energies bought in in the special year of 2012 created a framework so strong that the support system is in place for amazing energies that will raise the consciousness of all humanity to a new level. A new level of awareness and understanding of what is being made available to them, of what their purpose and path in this lifetime holds for them, for the love of God that there is within each and every one of us to enable all of this to unfold in the most glorious and beautiful way.

The love and light of God which passes all understanding, which is within each fibre, cell, breath of your existence, encourages and enables you all to step up into these energies, into the light and love, and into the higher dimensions of the glorious place that awaits us all.

And in this space, this opportunity that is made available to us, linking to the ancient knowledge and wisdom of Atlantis, and Lemuria, we can regain this balance and harmony in all things for the betterment of all.

Remaining in the higher energies of love, remaining in a state of grace is not always an easy state to retain, it is challenging, and requires the intention of honesty, openness, change, release and focus, but when you aspire to this higher level of perception, when you aspire to keep the balance of all things in perspective, when you allow in the light and love of God, then you can achieve this state of grace, this state of balance and harmony.

balance and harmony

Reading these words and absorbing these energies will assist you in perceiving how this state feels, how marvellously this state of grace allows you to keep that balance, that glorious state of love. Once you have experienced this state of grace and love, then you will wish to aim for or aspire to this place of being.

For when you are on that high wire, you can see things from a higher perspective, you can see all around you, the Earth, all living beings, the skies, the heavens; you are at one with All That Is, you are part of the elements of existence, you are part of the very core of life itself, and so maintaining that balance, focus and consideration becomes part of who you are.

And just as the high wire expert practices his craft, practises his balance and his focus and his strength and dedication because he aspires to complete his task and aim for success, then so too can all humanity aspire to keep, maintain and enjoy the state of balance and harmony with all things, within themselves, within their beings, within their physicality, within their heart, within their minds and in all that they do, say, think and have intentions for.

And so, dear ones, we leave you with the image of dedication, practise, aspiration and finally success in

completing your intention of balance and harmony in all ways, all levels and all dimensions, and know that we are here for you, at all times, to seek guidance, support, encouragement, love, acceptance and acknowledgement, so until time again.
Our greatest love to you all."

Connecting to the Christ Consciousness
An Elestial Crystal Communication

"The golden energy in my form which links to the golden ray of light and love links you to the Christ consciousness energies.

Encapsulated in my form are the structure and energies and intentions to assist you to open your heart to these energies, to reconnect to the sun God RA, life giving force of All That Is, and all the wisdom and knowledge carried through to the times of Thoth and Horus.

For as all these ages and stages pass in your human lifetimes, so the energies are formed and held within the crystal form which evolves within the Earth.

And can one form posses such power, such creativity, such connectivity? And the answer is yes, it can, for crystals are another gift from God to help you all at this exciting time on Earth.

As the Plan unfolds, as all that has been put in place for this time now begins to become reality, as your connection to the Christ light expands, as ancient knowledge and wisdoms are released, so your crystalline structure opens and expands, and your heart expands to integrate the love that is available to you.

As you hold or visually link into this crystal energy form, so you are strengthening your connection to all the aspects of life giving energy, of Christ light, of love, and light, the composition of the colour gold, the energy of the word itself, all contribute to the sense of expansion and integration of the new Golden Age of Enlightenment.

As you connect to these energies, so your consciousness expands beyond its limited human mind set to include the universal opportunities and possibilities that await you all in this new dimension.

Expand your thinking to beyond what you think is possible in this paradigm, and be open to magical possibilities that await all humanity in the next level of existence and reality.

This is truly a time for limitless expansion, and we follow your progress to this Golden Age, a golden time of peace and abundance across all times, levels and dimensions.

Amen, dear ones, Amen."

Opening Your Heart Centre
A Powerful Meditation from The Crystal Team

For this meditation you will be working with a crystal so please choose one which you feel drawn to. Once you have selected a crystal hold it, feel its texture, and talk to it about your intention to open your heart to the love that is available to you. Release any accumulated energies the crystal may have by blowing gently on it and asking it to release all that is no longer required.

Hold it in your left hand and place your left hand over your heart area, then place your right hand over this.

Take some gentle deep breaths and as you do so relax your mind and body, feel your energies linking to the loving energies of Mother Earth.

Invite the protection of the crystal beings to surround you and make your connection to the heavens.

Focus on the energy of the crystal next to your heart, feel the energy and the love of God radiating through this crystal bringing you closer to Source, bringing you closer to the fount of All That Is, the provider of all your experiences, the provider of your soul purpose at this time.

Feel the petals of your heart gently open to receive this love energy.

Feel the connection of the crystal energies to Mother Earth who is the provider of your physical experiences, the provider of your home and sustenance in this lifetime.

Feel these connections growing and expanding in waves of love and light flowing around your heart and out into your aura, growing and expanding, and merging with your soul friends here on Earth.

Know that you will always be connected on this energetic level, and know that your heart has expanded exponentially to receive the light and love of God, the angels, Archangels, and all other forms of energy essence to support you on your joint and individual journeys.

Gently close the petals of your heart and seal it with a golden rose knowing you can return at any time, and we leave you with our greatest love and joy for all time. Amen."

Take a few deep breaths, open your eyes, and feel your feet firmly on the ground, and enjoy a glass of water to refresh you after this beautiful meditation.

Insights on Colours of Light

"Rainbows are the colours of light that link Heaven and Earth; they delight the heart, soul and mind as they arc from Earth through to join the two worlds together.

The colours of the rainbow are the colours of the chakras of your own physicality and those of the Earth, the colours representing the emotional, physical, mental and spiritual aspects of yourself, of Mother Earth with Heaven; the colours that represent the energies of your energy centres, and those of Mother Earth which regulates your beingness, regulates that of Mother Earth.

In linking the colours of your chakras and the colours of the Earth chakras, you are blending your energies and those of Mother Earth into a connection, a link that unites as one, unites as the rainbow bridge linking those energies to Heaven. So the oneness and unity of the energies of the chakras of humanity and of the planet combine as one to link with the oneness of All That Is.

This image, this visualisation, demonstrates another aspect of the oneness of All That Is, another layer if you like, of the way that all humanity is linked, and how all humanity is linked with Mother Earth, and also this combination is linked to the energies of God.

This image represents once again that there is no separation; there is no difference between life on Earth and life in Heaven. It is all one dear ones, it is all one.

the Rainbow children

The energies of your loved ones are around you, the energy of Christ the son of God, is around you, the energy of God is around you. All this is within your energy; it is all part of you as part of the oneness of all that exists within your orbit. When you see a rainbow, you can see the link, it is a reminder for your conscious mind when you see rainbows in crystals, when you see colours of light shown in other forms, they are all signs and reminders of the link and connection between the two worlds. There is no separation; the rainbow lifts the veil for a glimpse of that energy.

The rainbow, to many souls on Earth, is a sign that their loved ones in spirit are connecting with them, and this confirms the ability of the energy of the colours of light to appear in many guises to remind you of that connection, and once you are aware of this, you will see many more ways in which these colours of light will appear in many, many forms and this will gladden your heart, this will lift your spirits and confirm that the connection exists.

And when we say lift your spirits what do we mean by this? We mean it will lift your spiritual energy, the energy within you that knows all of this, the knowledge and wisdom that exists within your subconscious minds, that exists within your cellular structure that exists within the very heart of your being. So seeing a visible sign of a rainbow within the sky, within a crystal or in another form, will lift that spiritual energy that resides in you that knows this that wishes to expand this awareness that wishes to grow within your beingness.

And so as the new children entering your orbit are called Rainbow children they are the spiritual energy that is the colours of light, that are here to bring about the connection of Heaven and Earth, to dispel the illusion of separation, to help the awareness grow within all humanity. Their spiritual energy is such that they will radiate this knowledge and wisdom from their very being for people to absorb and remember and recall and integrate until all people have reconnected to their true selves, their true spiritual energy, their true being as part of the oneness of All That Is.

the colours of unity and love

And children generally delight in rainbows, they know within their being that they are special, they recognise the energy of these colours of light; they love the feeling of connection it brings.

And these colours as we have said represent the colours of light, the colours of the love and light of God for you to see in a visual sense, to see in a form that your conscious brain will accept. As you accept seeing them in crystals and in other forms, so you are taking in more of this light and love of God, the colours of oneness, the colours of unity and love.

And so these colours that represent also your chakra colours, that represent those of Mother Earth, blend the energy of emotional, spiritual, mental and physical into one beingness of love and light, blending the energies of your energy systems into one flowing energy, into one universal energy of love and light.

And as this energy flows around your orbit, as it flows around your world, so it brings in the love and light of God, it allows the universal flow of energy to bring peace, love, compassion, sanctity, harmony, joy, clarity, happiness, equality, fairness and grace to all living beings to Mother Earth and beyond in the most magnificent way.

Enjoy your colours of light, enjoy your connection to spirit, enjoy the glow as your spiritual energy flows and grows and expands with the universal energies, with the light and love of God, for we are here for you all at all times, as we move forwards into the new era, the new dawn of times here on planet Earth.

Adieu dear ones, adieu with many rainbow blessings."

Blessings of Love

"Our gift to you as always, dear beloved souls, is one of love. In times of heartache and difficulty, we are here for you always, feel our love envelop you in its softness and its grace, and know we are here for you to access at any time of day and night.

In your darker hour, we are here for you, and in the light hours of day we are here for you, so call on us and feel our love and appreciation for all your experience
now and forever more. Amen."

The Pink and Silver Flame

"The Pink and Silver Flame is a very special gift which is being shared at this time for all those who are ready to understand the intention and purpose of its creation.

As you know pink is the colour energy of love, think of the rose quartz crystal energies of unconditional love and infinite peace, hold this energy to your heart and feel the warmth, the softness, the gentleness of this energy warming your heart, dissolving any energetic imbalances, miscreations, misdeeds or other unnecessary blockages.

Feel its warmth and softness melt through any resistant feelings and thoughts, any stubborn resistance that may remain, and allow the love to flow through your heart and flow around your body, and fill all your senses and structures with pure love.

And then focus on the silvestre colour, the colour of light, the colour of purity and innocence, of renewal and restoration and new beginnings and possibilities, and allow this thought and energy to fill your consciousness and your heart with freshness and hope and compassion and clearance and lightness. See it clearing and bringing in scope and potential for new emotions, new ideas, new ways of perception and beingness.

And put the two colours together in a Pink and Silver Flame and offer it to all those who you feel are ready to appreciate this strong yet subtle force.

For those who wish to move forwards, who wish to move into the higher energies, who wish to see and understand the bigger picture, who wish to be heart-centred and bigger hearted, who wish to see and understand the pain of others whilst not taking on this pain yet just accepting and understanding and allowing and knowing it is their journey, offering the Pink and Silver Flame allows you to offer a great gift for their selves to accept, to take, absorb, integrate and use to clear their own energetic imbalances, miscreations, misunderstandings, misdeeds and collective imbalances through ancestral lines and this lifetime and future lifetimes.

You are understanding their pain and their desire to move through this pain and have great compassion for their suffering; and yet in offering such loving energies you know that you can assist them to feel such love as to be able to clear and release these issues and aspects, and so are offering a great gift of love, compassion, clearance, positivity, hope, clarity and joy.

And for yourself, dear ones, you can invoke the Pink and Silver Flame of love and compassion, for love starts with love for ourselves. See yourself within this Flame, have compassion for yourself, feel the love that flows through this compassion, feel the warmth, the generosity of love, the strength of the love that is available to you to dissolve and melt all that which no longer serves you, and take in the optimism, hope, renewal that allows you to move forwards with expectation, joy, clarity, understanding and wisdom, refreshed and renewed across all times, levels, and dimensions.

See the Pink and Silver Flame assist Mother Earth to cleanse and release all her aspects as she continues on her journey. See her held strongly and lovingly within these energies of love and compassion, and see her absorb and relish in the energies of renewal and regeneration across all times, levels and dimensions.

And see all living beings within the Pink and Silver Flame, see them all healthy and glowing and happy, refreshed and renewed across all times, levels and dimensions.

And when you see or hear of anything which is not in alignment with the highest and greatest good of all, you may wish to offer the Pink and Silver Flame of love and compassion to that situation or event.

For, all intentions of good intent are a significant contribution to the whole, and as we are all part of the whole this will benefit all people and all living things, the stars, the galaxies and beyond.

So use the Flame wisely, in accordance with your intuition, and know that you are making a significant contribution to the clearance and cleansing of old stuck energies and allowing in the love, compassion and awareness that creates the opportunity for renewal and restoration.

This is all in accordance with the Divine Plan laid down for you all, and is in accordance with the Divine wishes for your future happiness and well-being, and that of Mother Earth, and all living beings and beyond.

It is our dearest wish that you embrace this gift within your hearts, minds, souls and beingness for the benefit of all humanity, across all times, levels and dimensions now and forever more Amen.

Our greatest love to you all till time again."

Maintaining Soul Connections

"Throughout our lives on Earth, there may be occasions when the physical body requires rest and 'time out' of the earthly plane, there may be times when the mental and emotional bodies of our physicality require restoration and renewal, and towards the end of our time on Earth the physical and mental aspects of our being may begin to weaken and withdraw.

Dementia is one such state of beingness where it can be challenging to remain in contact with the person to give reassurance, love and continuity. Physical ailments, comas and other situations also present the same challenges.

All physical beings manifest on Earth to learn what they chose to learn and experience what they chose to experience, and sometimes real life gets in the way of fulfilling these aspects but whatever the outcome we are all spirit in essence, we are all sparks of light and love of God, we are all beings of love in the true sense of the word. It is this aspect that we can connect with; the soul energy and soul essence that enables us to connect at a deep level to provide love, gratitude, appreciation, encouragement, acceptance, forgiveness and support. It is the oneness of All That Is that enables us to connect with all beings on a soul level.

love is the greatest form of healing

And so sit quietly, tune in to your heart centre and fill your heart centre with love. Request permission from the higher being of the person you wish to connect with, and if granted you can tune in on a soul level with the intention of sending love to that person.

Intention, dear ones, is the important aspect, for intention, when correct and right in its energies, allows for energy to follow thought and for the connection to be made on a soul level. Incorrect intentions are not permissible under God's Law.

So allow the connection with All That Is to flow into the soul of the person, and send them love, for love is the greatest form of healing available. Allow beautiful soft pink light to flow through their being, allow the energies of love and compassion to flow freely though their energy field.

Send thoughts of support, gratitude, thankfulness, joy, peace, whatever feels appropriate in the rightfulness of God's Law, and know that the soul of that person will receive these thoughts and intentions, and this will be of great value, reassurance, and will be appreciated on all times, levels and dimensions.

All souls are linked in unity, all souls are here on Earth to grow, expand and understand the fullness of the light and love of God as part of God's wholeness, and all thoughts of love benefit all souls across all times, levels, and dimensions, so your thoughts of love add to the love quotient of all living beings, Mother Earth and beyond.

End your connection with love and reassurance as part of the commonality of all souls, and know that you can return and make the connection again.

Bring yourself back into your own energy, give thanks for this opportunity to connect with your loved one, and enjoy the knowledge that you have contributed to the love quotient of All That Is for the benefit of all.

With our greatest love."

Blessings of Love and Compassion
I have compassion for your distress

Insights on the Animal Kingdom (Cats)

"Cats are another valuable asset to the world in general and to humans in particular. As part of the cycle of life, as part of the oneness of All That Is, they are created as an integral part of the wholeness. Each being on Earth has its own role to play, its own lessons to learn, and its own reasons for experiencing life on Earth.

And within this individual role and purpose there are layers of other roles and purposes within the matrix of life on Earth as a totality, and life in the universe in general. For as you are beginning to understand and accept we are all part of the love of God, all created in God's image and all part of the love that God has and shares for all his creations, and understanding; this will help all people accept and realise the need and the beauty of working with all living beings as they have so much intelligence, knowledge and wisdom to share that will add to the human's experience on Earth, and their enjoyment of life in general.

Being at one with all living beings is a gift beyond measure for the love, peace, humility and grace it brings to all, and the peace and harmony that it creates on Earth; and it will help peace descend on Earth as part of the Plan when all souls recognise this. For the slaughter of animals to supply the needs of greed, false glamour and miscreations, does not add harmony to the energies of life on Earth, it perpetuates the energetic imbalances and goes against the laws of nature, and so creates disharmony, not harmony, among all living beings.

The animal kingdom suffers for these miscreations, and their pain and loss and struggle for survival is not in accordance with the highest and greatest good of all including mankind, so the work and demands of a few upset the balance for the whole.

the world of cats

So returning to the world of cats within the overall picture, they have their own purpose and path and unlike dog spirits have not determined to be in service in the same way, but are still in service in their own way as part of God's creations. They have agreed to be domesticated to some extent to live with humans to bring peace, solace, love and comfort, and at the same time to retain that independence to roam at will; as part of the larger family of cats they need to be free to roam, spreading their light and love within their area.

They also have inner intelligence and use this to find their way home; their senses are highly developed and tuned into the natural world. They communicate with other animals, insects and Mother Earth, through various means of communication and can detect imbalances within the Earth's surface. It is no surprise that they have favourite places to go to, favourite places to rest, and these are often on specific areas of the Earth where they can make a connection, and send healing to the Earth and its surrounding living beings.

Cats are designed to be restful enjoying many hours of sleep and rest; they bring peacefulness and love through their energy fields and calmness to those in need of relaxation and solace.

And all this is done through an advanced energy system that senses energetic imbalances within the Earth and within humans, and as such are able and happy to rest for longer periods in these areas to bring about the necessary restoration of balance and peace.

They are designed to be appealing so that they are welcomed into homes, and are lovable and domesticated so that they can carry out their work as necessary, for remember dear ones, nothing happens by chance, and so cats are by design appealing and exhibit characters and characteristics that make them welcome as pets. And you may think this is obvious, but it is not obvious that creatures who have volunteered to do this work, to be in homes, to bring love and peace and harmony, would necessarily be packaged in a form so acceptable as the domestic cat.

cats are healers

The energy work that these pets are able to do is a wonderful part of the healing work as energy clearance and restoration as part of the whole picture. Animals can sense and hear and pick up on many aspects of human activities and emotions, and it is now being understood, accepted and welcomed that animals can communicate back to us. How amazing is this? That not only are they healers, peace bringers, comforters and bringers of joy and happiness, they can also impart information to us which is of great benefit to humanity and individual cat homers - we do not use the word owners – as humans cannot own the souls of animals as one person cannot own the soul of another person, but humans can be caretakers or co-partners in life especially when they understand the wonderful work and benefits that cats bring to the world.

This communication ability will grow to become of great significance, for as humans accept that the Earth too is a living being, as Mother Earth has her own journey and path, as she too suffers from man's miscreations, then the more information that becomes available to humanity on how to live in peace and harmony, how to respect all living beings, how to bring peace on Earth, then the greater the benefit to individual people and humanity as a whole.

For once again, we repeat, that there is no separation between beings, between Mother Earth and living beings, there are physical forms, personalities, identities, characteristics and so on, but you are all part of the same creation in different manifestations and will realise, respect and welcome the information available to you from these different life forms.

ancient and sacred wisdom

Your understanding of this knowledge and information, the ancient and sacred wisdom of the Earth people, the animal kingdom and all living beings will help bring balance and harmony, joy, respect, honour and love to you all on Earth.

Be open to receiving communications from all aspects of life, be open to the generosity of all life forms for the wonderful work they continue to do as part of keeping the balance, providing beauty, joy, happiness and healing energies for the whole.

Be open to the exciting new ways of living that become available when you open your heart centre to all of this, and know that you are helping to create joy, harmony and above all peace on Earth for this is your birthright, this is your homecoming, this is your future.

Enjoy all the aspects dear ones, and be grateful for all the gifts that are being made available to you at this exciting time on Earth. Enjoy your contact and communication with cats and thank them for their service work as we thank you for yours. With our greatest love as always in this expansion of knowledge and awareness; till time again, adieu dear ones adieu."

Time for Reflection for the New Year Ahead

"Make yourself comfortable at a time when you will not be disturbed. Take some deep breaths allowing yourself to relax with each breath. Feel your connection with Mother Earth and know that she will hold you in her loving energies during this time. You may wish to invite in your preferred essence of protection …

It is of great benefit to spend some time in contemplation of the past year; for some it may have been a challenging year testing your ability to remain within the energies of light and love, and we commend you all for your endeavours and acceptance of these situations. For as you understand, this is your learning and so to progress on your journey you are given new opportunities to raise your game, to raise your level of service, and to see how magnificently you put into practise all that you have learnt. And some of these challenges have tested you to the limit in many ways, and we are amazed and in awe of your dedication and commitment.

So perhaps dear ones you would like to spend a few moments reflecting on how much you have achieved, how much you have raised your awareness, increased your commitment to each other and to your service work, how much you have helped many others, for rest assured you have not only assisted many, many people but you have raised the awareness and the intention of a multitude of souls, and have assisted in healing many souls and Mother Earth herself.

So please reflect and commend yourselves for all that you have achieved.

Forgive yourself for any thoughts, actions, deeds or other where you may feel you were not successful in keeping your balance.

Love yourself for where you are now compared to where you were a year ago.

Give thanks to all those who have helped you.

Forgive those whose actions may have caused you pain, and thank them for the lessons they are bringing to your attention for clearance.

Thank all spirit forms who have been with you in countless ways – some you have recognised, and many you have not noticed.

And enjoy a few moments of reflection for all your magnificence.

And now we can look ahead to the coming times to the approach of the new era, the new Golden Age.

See within your heart which qualities you may still wish to work on, and acknowledge that as an aspect for your awareness.

See where you feel within your heart that you would like to spend more time, and how this can manifest for the good of yourself and others.

See yourself joyfully fulfilling this aspect of your life.

See your physicality as healthy, whole and happy; see if there are any areas you may wish to focus on in order to maintain that physicality in optimum balance in order to live your life to the full.

See all your chakras glowing, radiating, healthy and balanced, bringing in more light and love, more joy and happiness, more clarity, creativity and understanding.

See all your beings linked as part of the oneness, part of the magnificent wholeness of All That Is, and know that you are an equally essential part of that whole.

Glory in the connectedness and the oneness yet with your own unique spark of being to create your own experience.

Call in your own guide and see if there is a special message for you now.

Bring all these aspects together, recall any insights and messages, and repeat to yourself:

I now resonate with All That Is across all times, levels and dimensions now and forever more Amen. The glory of the love and light of God is within me as I am part of it.

Slowly come back into your awareness, and note anything significant for yourself.

Adieu, dear ones, Adieu."

See Love in All Things
An Elestial Crystal Communication

I am the universal crystal of peace and love.
Love through every heartbeat, through every sight and sound.
Love through every sunrise and sunset.
Love through the dawn chorus, and through the sun's rays.
Love through a smile, and a gesture of kindness.
Love through harmony in all things, and with all things.
Love through every flower and tree.
Love through the heart centre of all beings
united as one heartbeat in the name of God
the fount of all love, the very being of love.
I am the universal crystal of love and peace for all times
in all dimensions, in all levels of beingness
now until evermore. Amen"

Your Right of Passage
A Rainbow Crystal Communication

I am the universal being of truth and honesty,
of love and forgiveness.
See my light shine brightly and clearly
guiding you to the light, dear ones, towards the light.
I am the being of love and forgiveness;
the two greatest attributes to aspire to.

A love so strong it unites you to all others,
through the heartbeat of love
linking you to the heartbeat of Mother Earth
and to the heartbeat of all other planets
throughout the universe and beyond.

The being of love and forgiveness
that creates a love so strong
to clear all those elements that no longer serve you,
to clear all those elements that prevent you from seeing the
light and the truth,
the clarity, honesty, openness and light that is there for you all,
dear ones, indeed it is there for you all.

I am the universal being of light, of clarity.
See the light, so bright and clear,
leading you into the realms of Heaven
where a love awaits you that is eternal and endless.
See my light shining, clearing all that no longer serves you
from your crystalline grid, your DNA

and your cellular structure
allowing the light and love of God to radiate throughout your being
for all to see and wonder at.

I am the universal heartbeat of all
that is linking you to the heartbeat of God
the love and light of the greatest being
the fount of All That Is.
Feel my energy, and absorb and integrate it into your being
and allow it to flow through you with joy and the glory of God.

I am the universal being of All That Is
enabling you to create love, harmony and joy,
enabling you to link to the energies of Heaven and Earth
and allow the light and love of God to enter your being
and flow through your chakras, clearing, cleansing, balancing
and harmonising
all your aspects of your beingness
and bringing you further into the light and love
of God and the heavenly realms.

All this is available to you all, dear ones. All this is available
should you wish to claim it as your right of passage,

With our greatest love for all times."

Intention and Purpose

"We wish to communicate, dear ones, that a life of balance and harmony can be the most wonderful state in which to experience your chosen existence in a physical form, in this lifetime, here on Earth at this exciting time.

For when you can accept that you are here because you have chosen to be here at this pivotal time in your soul growth, and in the soul growth of your home and provider, Mother Earth, then it makes it a lot easier for you to understand your reason for your being here, and the intention and purpose of your actions whilst on this earthly plane.

When you are able to stand back and think, yes, now I can begin to see the bigger picture, I can begin to understand a greater purpose than my own existence as a solitary unit in this lifetime, then you can begin to make the reconnection to all your inherent wisdom and knowledge that you have bought with you in your crystalline grid, your DNA, and your cellular structure.

For when you accept that you are on a journey, and this is only one stage of that journey, then you can open up to all the previous experiences that you have had in other lifetimes; all the knowledge and wisdom that you have gained during these periods of soul growth, and so can benefit from that perspective, that understanding, knowledge, perception, awareness and appreciation.

we are all energy

And in understanding all of this you are instantly in a different energy, an energy that creates opportunities and potentialities for you to grow in that energy, to expand your soul essence, to strengthen your connection to Source, and to develop your inner being in accordance with your desire to experience life in a physical form at this exciting time, along with the multitude of other souls who also chose to be in the earthly orbit at this time.

And in making these connections within your inner core being you will recall your previous life and energy experiences in Lemuria and Atlantis where life was lived within the energies of balance and harmony.

For being in this state, is very much an energy state, for we are dear ones all energy, and as such can choose which energy state we wish to experience. And drawing on our core knowing of how it feels to be living in a state of balance and harmony, to be at peace within one's being, to be at peace with all others, with all living beings and Mother Earth, is a natural state that you have experienced and have elected to experience again within the earthly plane.

The ethos of life in those times had the basic understanding that all things worked together, all things, all living beings were equal and of equal value, and all beings have a role to play in maintaining a state of balance and harmony for the benefit of all.

the Lemurian experience

The Lemurian existence was very gentle, unsophisticated and pure, these high vibrational beings chose to experience a very simple lifestyle on Earth; they lived very lightly on the Earth and left little evidence of their existence. Originating from the energies of Orion, Sirius, The Pleiades, and

Neptune, they came to Earth to experience life on this planet and had a deep love and respect for her.

She was providing them with a home, shelter, sustenance and a place of such beauty that they respected, loved, honoured and appreciated all that was being made available to them. They held a deep desire to work with her energies to maintain balance and harmony in all aspects of life and thus allow her to continue, unaffected by outside negative energies, in her own soul journey and fulfil her contract and her purpose as part of the universal energies for, do not forget dear ones, as mentioned before that Mother Earth is one planet among your solar system, and that is but one small part of the universe, and damage to the energy balance of Mother Earth will have ramifications in the balance and harmony of other aspects of space.

The Lemurians also desired to assist Mother Earth and created the Lemurian crystals within the Earth, which allowed for deep healing to be sent into the Earth. This beautiful well-intentioned healing energy would be held within the powerful crystals and then directed to where it was needed and when the optimum time for that healing to be accepted was determined also by the crystals.

advanced crystal technology

The crystal technology being so advanced that these aspects of awareness and knowledge are still not understood in the human field today but as more of you advance and as more of your intentions exhibit a desire to create balance and harmony, peace and goodwill, then more information will be revealed and our dear ACM; will be detailing more of this information as time advances within your perception of time.

Rest assured dear ones, that crystal technology will play a significant part in the future of all humanity as we approach critical mass and the energies of love and light become ever more powerful.

So more on crystal technology later, dear ones, but for now do understand that these crystals are working within the Earth transmitting knowledge and information within the Earth, and externally to the outer reaches of space, as part of the unfolding of the Divine Plan, and we appreciate those who join together in their groups to link into these Lemurian crystal energies to send this loving and powerful healing to Mother Earth, and we request as much of this healing as you can unite in sending in order to assist your beautiful planet in clearing and cleansing all that is no longer relevant for her to take forward into the new era, the new dawn of times.

And so dear ones, link into your ancient knowledge and wisdom, reconnect to your previous energy experiences of the Lemurian lifetimes, recollect the feelings of glory, peace, beauty, recollect the desire to be at one with all things, all living beings, and especially within yourself. Recollect the higher energy experiences when our intentions are of the highest level, when your perceptions are of the well-being of all, when your heart leads you to be at one with all things in love, appreciation, acceptance, peace, faith, trust and honouring all around you.

Recollect the state of grace of being in balance and harmony with all things and bring this forward into your being now, into your consciousness, and into your daily breath, your daily beingness, and glory at all that is being made available to you to assist you in this journey.

Till time again, with our greatest love."

Creative Solutions
A Lemurian Crystal Communication

"The Lemurian way of life was simple, peaceful and joyful. The emphasis was on a spiritual existence which is why, as has been indicated before, they chose not to have the sophisticated technology exhibited by the Atlanteans. They chose to focus their time and endeavours into peaceful thoughts and activities that assisted their own growth, that of others and the well-being of all for the highest and greatest good. And in this respect they enjoyed much creative activity and working with the soil, with the elements and with Mother Earth.

Their innate intelligence and understanding of how things work, their level of awareness enabled them to live very constructive, satisfying and fulfilling lives as they had much understanding of science, technology and physics as you refer to these elements. But they chose not to bring too much of this energy with them, but to retain enough to allow for the major constructions built under their management, and for sophisticated agricultural methods which ensured that all people were well fed and nourished.

Again as has been said before, when there is no pollution, when the air is fresh and clean, crops will grow more healthily and the beneficial effects on the human body are much greater. The waters were regularly blessed and given due gratitude and added to the lack of pollution; they were of crystal clear freshness and so the crops were watered by this beautiful life-giving element in the most beautiful way too.

balance and appreciation

Their innate knowledge allowed for the most sophisticated irrigation systems using the moon energy and the sun energy to work and maintain these systems which were simple yet very effective in using all natural elements to create and keep them working effectively.

The timing of the planting done in accordance with meditation, natural cycles and prayers were adapted each year with the awareness and knowledge of taking all aspects into account and in conjunction with the energies of Mother Earth, for after all, it would be her energies and agreement which would mainly create for the well-being of the crops in accordance with other aspects of nature, so why would you not include her in your calculations?

And the needs of the land were considered so that the soil remained healthy and balanced and was not abused in any sense but was valued and appreciated for its bounty.

So can you get this sense of balance and appreciation, bringing in the energies of love, appreciation, abundance and harmony for all things, and can you see how the advanced awareness of their spiritual intention for the highest and greatest good of all worked to produce such abundant and healthy crops?

absorb the energy

And dear ones this is something that you can start to introduce to your lives now, you do not need to wait for governments to make or change laws, you do not need to wait for directives of any sort; you can start to get a sense of this in all aspects of your everyday life.

In your garden sit quietly, absorb the energy and beauty of what you see, listen to the sounds and sense what you feel, are there any plants that would do better off planted in a different place, are the colours balanced, are the energies balanced? Start to feel how the garden feels; start to be aware of the balance of energies; start to feel what the garden needs to flourish; start to think of alternatives to the chemicals that are used to feed the plants, are there natural alternatives, are there plants that when planted together feed each other, are there areas where certain types of plants grow better?

Really start and feel and sense the balance, the love, the harmony of the garden as one, albeit lots of manifestations of energies, but overall one energy that comes together in unity and glory, a masterpiece of nature.

Bring in the energies of the moon, think of the moonshine energies of a new or full moon casting their loving energies over the garden. Think of the rain, the nourishing rain that feeds the cells of the plants. Does your garden need some water features, some energies from colour, some balance of wood, or other natural materials; can some crystals bring light and love into your garden?

use your intuition

So sit dear ones and think and feel how beautiful your garden can be. Experienced gardeners work on an intuitive level and bring a balance, and even then there is more that can be created by thinking and feeling all of these things and giving thanks for all the beauty that is available, all the bounty and generosity of Mother Earth, and in all this you will think expansively and energetically about your garden in a way that was previously beyond your thinking and comprehension.

And however small your garden you will create something beautiful and harmonious which allows all aspects of nature, insects, butterflies, birds and so on to live, thrive, survive in harmony and balance for all times.

Enjoy this aspect dear ones, expand your current consciousness and be amazed at the results. And in the same way the Lemurians were able to create such masterpieces as the Banaue rice fields by listening to the sounds, by meditation and asking for help, by observing the contours of the land, and by using their innate wisdom, they were able to create such magnificent edifices that then supplied the population which could also be traded at markets for other commodities.

magnificent gifts await

Think carefully about the energies of what you buy, how was it made, is it sustainable, is it ethical, are the producers fairly treated, all these factors maintain the energy of your input and your intention to use only those things that comply with your intention for the highest and greatest good.

And in all these things you will create wonderful energies, and this is possible on small and grand scales when groups of people get together to work on allotments and projects.

Time, intention, purpose and love are required to create the bedrock of principle and manifestation and wondrous outcomes can be achieved.

As your level of understanding and awareness increase about the opportunities that were unavailable to you previously and are now open to you, you can avail yourself of these magnificent gifts and begin to create your own Heaven on Earth, and begin to demonstrate that there is another way, that things can change and life can improve beyond all measure, beyond your current imaginings and expectations. How great a gift is that dear ones, how great a gift indeed?

So do not be afraid to think differently, to be different and to forge ahead with the new energies of light and love, reconnecting to the beautiful energies of what you have experienced before, and what you know to be true.

Enjoy the journey of discovery dear ones, be excited and see what you can create in light and love for the greatest good of all."

Insights on the Animal kingdom (Butterflies)

"These beautiful creatures of light and love are sent to the earthly realm for the benefit of mankind, and for the successful maintenance of life on Earth. Their colour and beauty assist in drawing your attention to their presence, for their role is an important one and so must be protected.

Like all of life, they are part of the whole, part of the oneness of All That Is; part of God's gifts to you all to sustain life on Earth, and mankind will do well to remember that he is also part of the whole, and not the most important part, but one part of life. And all life must be kept in balance and harmony for all aspects to be allowed to play their part and to fulfil their function of life on Earth.

When one aspect of life becomes out of balance and tries to control other life forms for their own benefit, this cannot be a good thing for it immediately disrupts the balance of each part of life doing their work, and this causes a reaction among all life and ultimately no one aspect of life is fulfilling its function properly in accordance with God's law and the law of nature, and so the whole is then out of balance. For mankind to realise and accept that he is not king of the realm of God and to learn to work in harmony and balance with all things will allow the balance to be restored and for all aspects to fulfil their function, and for life to flow and exist beautifully in accordance with its intention and purpose.

Butterflies are a part of this wholeness, a beautiful, bright colourful part of the cycle of nature linking the energies of plants and wildlife with the building blocks of all life, all sounds, vibrations, all universal structures and essences working with nature, with the natural flow of the cycle of life and the seasons to connect, communicate and link messages and energies on many levels and dimensions, this unseen gift being a vital role in the continuation of all life.

Planned intention of thought

We celebrate the work being undertaken to raise awareness of this vital role and the intentions of those who seek to maintain a landscape that allows for this to continue.

And on another level, butterflies as with birds, can be messengers from Heaven, they can represent the spirits of souls of the departed, they can bring messages of love and joy and comfort to those who are open to them. Thinking of a loved one and seeing a butterfly are connections from loved ones who can suggest the thought and create the reality for that event to exist, for as we say, dear ones, that nothing happens by chance, and when you have a thought, it could be a connection is being made by the loved one first to help you be aware of the idea to actually take notice and then to see the gift they have sent you whether it be a number plate, a rainbow or butterfly or other personal message – you call it synchronicity – we call it planned intention of thought.

And again this strengthens your belief, it strengthens your connection, and it opens your heart centres to more of the love and light of God/Source who created all of this for you. God loves you all dear ones and desires for you all to be happy and to feel his love, for in love is peace, in love is balance and harmony, and in this way peace will return to Earth and balance and harmony will exist for all living beings, mankind and Mother Earth.

So enjoy seeing your beautiful butterflies, enjoy their flight, their brilliance and be grateful for their work as part of the cycle of nature under God's law, and pray for balance and harmony in all things.

Adieu dear ones till time again. Adieu."

A Meditation to Align You with the Love and Heart energies of God

"It is always our delightful intention to assist those souls on Earth to clear stagnant energies from past times, clearing the way for new lighter energies, new beginnings, new understandings and relationships for future generations.

Events in this lifetime can be adversely affected by events from the past, and clearing these enables people to live a life true to their soul path and purpose without hindrance from extraneous aspects that were imposed upon them as children.

And again we would remind you that this is the lifetime you have chosen to experience in this dimension at this time and Free Will enables you to think, say and act in ways which are not always in true alignment with the Source of All That Is – the love and heart energies of God.

And so we see this desire to clear and cleanse these energies enabling you all to move forward into the light and create a greater understanding and awareness, honesty and openness between you all, enabling you to enter your true light, to reconnect to your true soul essence within the light and love of God, fount of all.

And again we would remind you that it is not always appropriate to bring this clearing into effect for all families without their consent or discussion, asking permission of the higher selves of those concerned will guide you on the appropriate course of action or deferment of the clearing until a more opportune time.

★★★★★

And so we recommend that you create a sacred loving space, bring in the light with candles if you are indoors, or create an outdoor ceremony; so in essence choose somewhere appropriate and comfortable for yourself.

Connect yourself to the universal energies of love and light, feel the love entering your heart centre, see yourself being filled to capacity with the glorious love and light of God.

See this light filling your aura, filling all your senses, does it have an aroma, how does it feel to you?

Feel your aura expanded fully, shining and shimmering around your physical body.

Take some deep breaths and take this light deep into every cell of your body, let it fill every particle and every cell within you until you feel glowing within and without with the intention of the love of God, for peace, understanding, acceptance and openness.

Relish in this feeling, and when you are ready ask that all past accumulated energies pertaining to all your experiences within your family that are no longer relevant to who you are or who you wish to be, are cleared and cleansed NOW.

Now at this very moment in time, all karma, all stagnant energies, all memories, experiences and effects that are no longer relevant to any part of your being, are now cleared and cleansed for all time, on all levels, and in all dimensions.

Feel how refreshing this is, to be relieved of all those past experiences and effects that have troubled you through this timeframe, to be relieved of the burden of worry, guilt, stress, anxiety, unhappiness and sorrow, and for these energies to be replaced by joy, happiness, freedom, excitement, openness, honesty, inner peace and trust.

See yourself glowing with life and light, see your body filled with lightness and brightness, see yourself radiating the light and love to all your family, to all members of your related experiences in all lifetimes, in all dimensions, and on all levels.

Sit with this beautiful feeling of freedom to be yourself, unfettered by past memories, effects, causes which were not of your making, and ask for assistance for all members within your family to also be released from these burdens and effects if they so chose to accept this offer.

To see you all happy, open, honest, joyful and glowing with inner peace, and radiant with the inner peace, and radiant with the inner light of their soul essence.

Congratulate yourself for being willing to shed these misconceptions, burdens, guilt's and sadness's, and anticipate a better, brighter happy time for you all in future times.

Each of you has the ability to move fully into the light of God, to move into your full soul path and purpose in your own unique individual way, in your own timescale, as this is a truism that must be accepted and acknowledged for we are not at liberty to affect another person's journey through this adventure of life.

So we leave you now to enjoy this new positive lightness and openness, and watch with great delight to see how the future reveals its gloriousness to you.

We thank you for your good intention in this matter, and send our greatest love now and forever more."

Gradually become aware of the room around you, take some deep breaths, open your eyes, stretch and give thanks for the gifts being made available to you.

The Way Forward 2

PART II

Please join us in raising the energies on Earth as we move toward the prophesied time of Peace on Earth.

Circle of Love
Trinity Healing and Prayer Circle
Crystal Skull World Day
Centre for Peaceful Restoration, Recovery and Recuperation

Circle of Love

The Circle of Love was established for all those who wish to unite in the energies of love, bringing peace and clarity for all.

The Ho'oponopono Prayer is used in a daily meditation for 5 minutes or longer if you have the time, to release all ancestral miscreations and energetic imbalances that have been passed down through the generations of our own families, and other community histories. In releasing all that is no longer relevant to ourselves, or the current energetic intention for peace, it enables all people to move forward in joy, happiness, clarity and love.

Continuing this practise regularly is of immense benefit to yourself, to all living beings, and to Mother Earth, as this is now the time to clear and cleanse all misunderstandings, hurts, upsets, miscreations, and so on, so that we move into the new way of life on Earth of honesty, clarity openness, unity, oneness and peaceful community living.

Please join our Face book page on:
https://www.facebook.com/pages/Circle-of-Love/1428915594036130

Or join in whenever you can, and know that you are being of great service to all mankind.

With the Circle of Love we have the extended family of crystal beings who add their energies and personalities to the Circle.

'Hope' holds the energy for the Circle, and radiates the energies of optimism and positivity through his crystalline essence.

This is enhanced by the additional crystalline beings, and we thank all the crystal skull guardians who have put forward the names of their skulls, to add to the energetic intention of the Circle.

So together with the Circle members, the crystal beings and the words of the Prayer, the energetic intention created is enormous, and the larger the Circle becomes, the more the Prayer is repeated, and the number of crystal beings added to this Circle, then the result is powerful and enormously effective.

The Crystal Team wish to offer ...

"We thank you all for your contributions to this Circle, and see its energy radiating out through the crystal highway, and through all crystalline connections, creating love, peace and harmony in great measure.

We deeply thank you for your intention and endeavours as this Circle continues to expand magnificently."

Trinity Healing and Prayer Circle

The Trinity Healing and Prayer Circle was created with Katy Gostick as a means of uniting people in focus and prayer at certain times of the year.

A foundation group initially created the energy for this Prayer Circle, and this energy pot continues to expand as more people join in. The energy pot remains in existence continuing to radiate healing energies as the Circle unites once every 3 months for 21 days in that month.

The Trinity energy linking to the Father, Son and Holy Ghost brings in a very powerful energy for the Circle, and assists all members to strengthen their connection to Source. Additionally 21 days strengthens this concept; 2 + 1 = 3 which equals the Trinity energy, and assists in opening the heart centre of all those involved, to receive the love and gifts available to them.

At each new Circle opening, a special theme presents itself to coincide with the energies of the time, and Katy's beautiful Rose Essence energies provided the focus for the last Circle of 2014.

Please take a look at our Face book page, and if this resonates with you then please do join in.

https://www.facebook.com/groups/622412344474169/

Alternatively you can join the email list to receive updates on the next Circle, and the weekly update where members share some of the insights they have received in the meditation.

The meditation itself is approximately 20 minutes and Katy holds the energy of the Circle for this time, and unites all Circle members in one loving energy; a video is available to follow for the meditation or you may choose to follow your own meditation routine.

Although the suggested times to link in are 7 am and 7 pm, anytime is really appropriate as all energetic intentions are welcome, and join in for all long as you are able.

My thanks go to Katy★ for her joint endeavours in this amazing Circle, and to all those who enjoy participating in it, and all those who are yet to link in.

The Crystal Team wish to offer ...

"The TH&PC is of immense value and brings the energies of support, healing, cleansing and acceptance to all who enjoy being part of it. The additional theme for each Circle benefits the individual, and adds significantly to the energetic intention necessary at that time to move all humanity forward into the new era, the new dawn of times and the prophesied time of Peace on Earth. All groups who unite in positive, loving intention are playing their part in making Peace on Earth not only a possibility but indeed a reality, and we thank you all.

The Trinity energy adds significantly to uniting all members in the love of God and opening your heart centres to the wisdom of the ages, and the ancient knowledge that is carried forward through this and all generations, world without end. Amen."

★www.katygostick.co.uk E: katygostick@btinternet.com

Crystal Skull World Day

The Crystal Skull World Day was introduced in 2014 by a group of dedicated souls who are all linked by a love of all things crystal.

The original concept of joining together for 5 minutes to send healing energy to all living beings and Mother Earth, gained momentum, and a Council was created to develop this idea.

A Face book page evolved and as more souls joined in, a date was established for November 22 or 23 in different time zones, and ideas formulated for how to link in on the day.

A video was produced, and a website created, for people to share their experiences and photos of their crystal skulls.

The energy for this event grew rapidly from the very beginning until hundreds of people were involved as guardians, bringing together thousands of crystal skulls to unite on the day.

The first CSWD was an amazing success, and plans are now being drawn up for the 2015 CSWD. You can join in by visiting the website and reading more about this magnificent event and receive newsletters, and follow on Face book.

The Crystal Team wish to offer

"This amazing event, which was laid down eons of time ago, manifested in reality at this auspicious time on Earth in the most magnificent way.

The energetic intention established at the very moment that this idea became a reality, grew to a magnificent level at the time of the event, and this energy surge has changed the future for mankind in a very positive way.

The energy level set in 2012 has now been raised by this event, and all other significant events since that time, to a new level which allows in more of the light and love of God as part of the Divine Plan for humanity on Earth at this special time.

As we move toward the prophesied time of Peace on Earth, we deeply thank all those who followed the call to service to create this and all events, allowing more souls to unite in love, peace, harmony and oneness to move forward into the new era, the new dawn of times with love, clarity, openness, trust, peace and joy.

We thank you all, and look forward to the development of the crystal skull world family as it expands toward the next event in 2015. Thank you. Amen."

www.crystalskullworldday.com
https://www.facebook.com/groups/CrystalSkullWorldFamily/

Centre for Peaceful Restoration, Recovery and Recuperation

It is our intention to establish a Centre for Peaceful Restoration, Recovery and Recuperation for all those brave souls who have sacrificed so much on our behalf, through action in the field of global conflict.

We, the Healing and Spiritual Network team, formed a group in order to examine how best to support all those suffering from trauma, and this includes the families and loved ones, caused through action, injury, and ill health, and loss.

We have worked closely with relevant agencies and groups to determine the most efficient means of offering restoration, recovery and recuperation to all those in need, and so our vision to create a Centre for Peaceful Restoration, Recovery and Recuperation was created.

We have witnessed firsthand, the devastation caused through loss of a loved one in action, and this special year commemorating 100 years since the beginning of the 1st World War has highlighted just how many generations of families have, and continue, to suffer from the effects of trauma, loss and devastation to all concerned.

It is our intention that this Centre will be a community project, where all people who have suffered trauma through whatever means in their life, will be able to visit and receive solace and comfort from the beauty of the grounds, and being part of the Centre and its evolvement.

Our Blueprint will establish the foundation for this Centre, and for its replication around this country and even abroad, as the need for this is vast and worldwide.

Volunteers will be able to assist in a variety of ways, for example, with the garden project, where wholesome produce will be grown to provide nourishing food for attendees.

Assistance with the day-to-day running of the Centre, and with the Equine Programme, will also be an opportunity to be part of this innovative and far-reaching project.

The Information Pack is available to read on our website, and a Face book page gives regular updates on our progress.

Donations to secure the long-term funding of this Centre are welcomed, and we will do all in our power to see this Centre established, and its long-term future secured, in order to offer restoration, recovery and recuperation to all those brave souls who have sacrificed so much on our behalf.

Loved ones and families will be invited to spend time at the Centre to receive the support and recognition they deserve for their part, as their sacrifice and dedication often remain unrecognised and unsupported.

The 12 Core Element Programme will offer techniques for health and well-being; mindfulness meditation will demonstrate the benefits of quiet contemplation; healing modalities will provide support in the recovery process, and the Equine Programme will further expand man's long standing relationship with horses, as part of the overall recovery process.

On-going support, and visits to the Centre, will provide confidence and self-empowerment for all, and assist in rebuilding positive options, and reintegration to normal living.

We already have an extensive list of people wishing to be part of the Centre, and Open Days and special events will introduce specialists in their own fields to share their advice and wisdoms.

Enjoying the beautiful grounds, and its special ambience, will be of benefit to all; volunteers, visitors, groups and attendees, and all people are invited to be part of the Centre in whichever way resonates with them. Financial support, ideas, suggestions, offers of practical support, promotion of the Centre, developing eco-systems, horticulture, entertainment, fundraising, are some of the ways in which people may wish to support this Centre.

This will be an exciting; fulfilling and worthwhile project to be part of, as we work to support all those brave souls who have given so much over so many generations, that life may be lived as we choose to do so. It is our intention to do all we can to support those in need of restoration, recovery and recuperation, and please join us if you are drawn to do so.

Thank you.

https://www.facebook.com/groups/1558183771062498/
Centre for Peaceful Restoration
 E: centreforpeace@mail.com
 W.
www.centreforpeacefulrestorationrecoveryandrecuperation.org.uk
 W: www.healingandspiritualnetwork.co.uk

About Lindsay

Lindsay has evolved through the intervening years since her first book was published, and is now involved in many significant events which are part of the overall Mission for Peace on Earth.

She continues to update her website with information communicated to assist all humanity to understand the changes that are taking place, and how all souls can move to be in alignment with their own truth, and assist in fulfilling their path and purpose in this lifetime, as we move toward the new era, the new dawn of times.

Lindsay is dedicated to see the establishment of a Centre for Peaceful Restoration, Recovery and Recuperation as part of this Mission for Peace, and is part of a dedicated team, working under guidance, to see the establishment of this Centre at the earliest opportunity, (details of this Centre are included in part II of this book), and its establishment will play a vital role, along with other initiatives, for peace around the world.

Prayer Circles and groups, meditations and social media avenues are all offered to support all souls on their individual journey to clear all ancestral imbalances, miscreations, and hurts and pains, that must needs be cleared in order for all souls to move forward in love, clarity, honesty, openness, oneness and unity with All That Is across all times, levels and dimensions, world without end. Amen.

Join Lindsay in these groups to assist you on your journey to oneness, and alignment with your heart centred truth of what you inherently know to be true within the heart and mind of God. Amen.

Contact Lindsay

E: info@lindsayball.co.uk
W: www.lindsayball.co.uk
Follow Lindsay on Face book:
https://www.facebook.com/lindsay.ball.963

The Crystal Team: for regular updates from The Crystal Team follow:
https://www.facebook.com/groups/626782910751237/
The Crystal Team

Follow the Circle of Love on:

https://www.facebook.com/pages/Circle-of-Love/1428915594036130

Trinity Healing & Prayer Circle
https://www.facebook.com/groups/622412344474169/

Centre for Peaceful Restoration, Recovery and Recuperation
https://www.facebook.com/groups/1558183771062498/
Centre for Peaceful Restoration
   E: centreforpeace@mail.com
   W: www.centreforpeacefulrestorationrecoveryandrecuperation.org.uk
   W: www.healingandspiritualnetwork.co.uk

Acknowledgements

It is with joy and gratitude that this second book in The Way Forward series has been published, and I hope you all enjoy and benefit from it.

The book is dedicated to our beautiful planet and all who dwell upon her; and without her there would be no life on Earth for us to experience and grow spiritually within our total spirit life, so I acknowledge the part that Mother Earth plays for all of us, in this lifetime, here and now.

I dedicate the book to all who dwell upon her, as we are all part of the oneness of All That Is, and are all connected. We learn and share with each other, through many avenues, the experiences, challenges and joys of our lives on this amazing planet, and share the beauty of life on Earth at this exciting time.

So in dedicating the book to our home, shelter and supporter in terms of sustenance and beauty, and all those who dwell upon her, I acknowledge the role that everyone plays in the interconnectedness of life on Earth as we move toward the new era, the new dawn of times, and the prophesied time of peace on Earth.

Personally, I would also like to thank the other members of the Healing and Spiritual Network team, as we work together to establish the Centre for Peaceful Restoration, Recovery and Recuperation, and to see our vision, under guidance, become a reality to support all those suffering from trauma, through whatever means, and in particular those brave souls who have sacrificed so much that we may live as we choose to do so.

I thank my family and friends, and in particular Peter for his supporting role and patience, his love and acceptance of my service work, my two inspirational daughters for the lessons of life and love, and for everyone who has supported this book on its journey to completion.

To those who offered to read the book before publishing, to Mike Brown for his role in seeing it through to publication, and to all those who have encouraged me along the way.

Blessings and joy to all who read this book, may it bring you enlightenment, peace and love.

Thank you.

Review

"Dear Lindsay. I have just completed your manuscript. I thoroughly enjoyed every page within it and thank you so much for allowing me the privilege to be amongst the first to receive its wisdom.

Reading it has made me feel that I am doing everything right with how I feel, lead my life, my beliefs, practices and the questions I have. I think it is exactly what the world needs at the moment. It is written in an informative, easy flowing manner and everything is easy to understand and no expectations are made. A lot of material comes across with the reader thinking you should feel this, should feel that, completely overlooking the fact that intention is the key to it all.

I'm sure a lot of people expect fireworks or similar (so to speak) with their practice. I know that I used to feel this way but I now know that spirit is very subtle, we are all unique and that we have to be patient and observe, then when we least expect it a chance happening can mean so much whether it be animal, numerical etc... I think the main problem I had in the past was slowing down. Life is such a fast pace these days! I feel this is the main obstacle of modern day life.

Your book deals with this most effectively. At the moment I am very disheartened by the number of people who live in houses but have all stones and rocks as their garden. To me they are missing out on so much pleasure and ignoring Mother Earth completely."

Bronwyn Nelmes

Index

Angels	67, 69
Archangel Michael	16,20
Atlantis	27,44,96,133,143,168
Avebury	18,21
Blessings	65,98,127,150
Birds	67-69,83
Butterflies	175-8
Christ Consciousness	142-3
Compassion	152,155
Crop circles	19,86
Crystals	14,34,44,65,97,103
Crystal skulls	22,40,186
Dementia	173
Divine Plan	7,10,65,74,153
DNA	7,38,66,91
Dogs	126-131
Dolphins	81,82
Energy	23,124
Flowers	83
Free will	10,32,62
Glastonbury	14,23-4
God	15,22,29,59,115
Golden Age	12,23,38,47
Heart Chakra	23
Healing	113,150
Horses	54-56
Humanity	58,90,129
Integrity	29,30
Laughter	48,110
Lemuria	44,141,168,171
Lemurians	9,13,95,169
Love	.28,32,47,55,91,99,119,183
Meditations	24,145,178

Moon	66
Mother Earth	7,13,16,36,55,97
Mother Nature	42,68
Music	75-6
Names	62-5
Oneness	162
Pyramids	131
Peace	50,117,125,163,188
Prayers	54,106,184
Rainbows	88,101,111,146-9,164
Seahorses	92
Solar System	11
Stars	
Stonehenge	
The Crystal Team	8,17,21,
Trees	60,73,76
Universe	63,86
144 Crystalline Grid	18,25,30,44,117